50 BIKING HOLIDAYS

50 Scenic Routes to Pedal from
Old Monterey to the Golden Gate

(Based on a series from the *San Jose Mercury News*)

By
Joan Jackson

Fresno

1977

Library of Congress No. 77-89786
ISBN 0-913548-45-6

Printed in the United States of America
Valley Publishers, 8 E. Olive Ave., Fresno, CA 93728

ACKNOWLEDGEMENTS

Richard Wisdom, Cover Photo
Tom Daniels, Maps
Fred Matthes, Emil Edgren, Tom Williams,
Al Magazu, Dave Milton, Inside Photos
Based on a series from the *San Jose Mercury News*

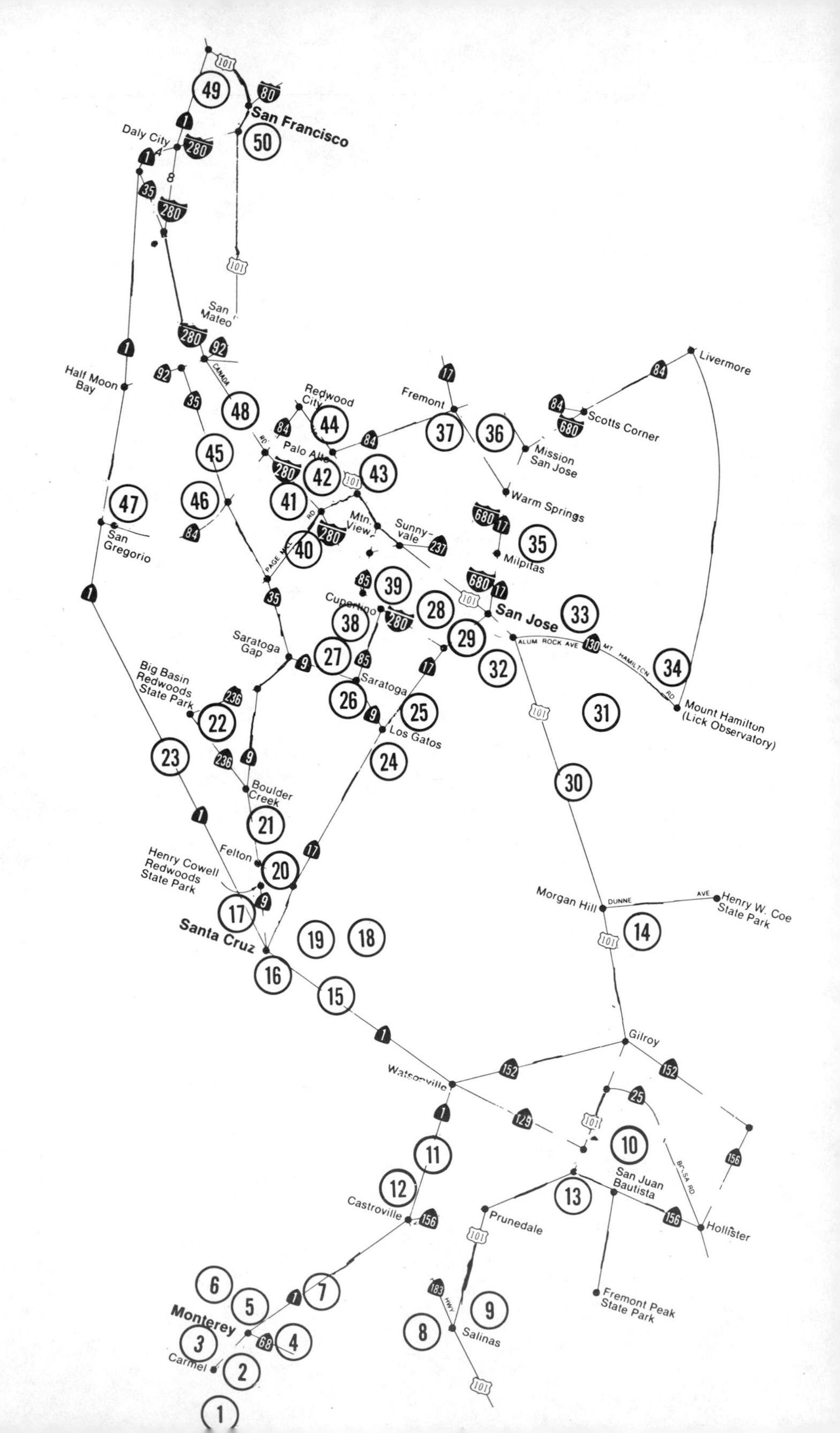

San Francisco
Daly City
San Mateo
Half Moon Bay
Redwood City
Palo Alto
Fremont
Livermore
Scotts Corner
Mission San Jose
Warm Springs
Mtn. View
Sunnyvale
Milpitas
San Jose
San Gregorio
Cupertino
Saratoga Gap
Saratoga
Big Basin Redwoods State Park
Los Gatos
Mount Hamilton (Lick Observatory)
Alum Rock Ave
Mt. Hamilton Rd
Boulder Creek
Felton
Henry Cowell Redwoods State Park
Santa Cruz
Morgan Hill
Dunne Ave
Henry W. Coe State Park
Gilroy
Watsonville
Castroville
Prunedale
San Juan Bautista
Bolsa Rd
Hollister
Monterey
Carmel
Salinas
Fremont Peak State Park
Page Mill Rd

BIKING HOLIDAYS

to "Daddy Bear" —
hope you enjoy
pedaling some of these to
keep in shape
Joan Jackson

TABLE OF CONTENTS

Let's Go Biking!

Dust off that 10-speed in the garage and get ready to see Central Coast California fueled by some of those calories you have been storing up all winter. From San Francisco south to Carmel is some of California's most beautiful biking country.

From the back of a bike you can feel the wind in your hair, taste the salt sprays off the ocean. Trails cut through redwood forests and follow the paths Indians once trod to the Missions; routes edge the ocean where the winds blast down the coast like a moon rocket exhaust and only the seagulls witness that you get off to walk your bike up the last hill.

You can go for a day, a week, or a month. These routes are one-day rides, plotted for easy riding plus the scenic views and points of interest. Ambitious riders can work out their own logistics, stringing together a number of rides for long distance treks. For the novice weekend biker—start easy and take along the entire family. Hills are fun, even if you have to get off and walk most of them.

Most bikes will do on these trails, although the kind kids ride with balloon tires make the pedaling awfully hard. The best all-purpose bike for weekend riding is the 10-speed because it is lightweight and has enough gears to allow you to climb inclines. The routes were chosen with the 10-speed in mind, although many can be done with a 3-speed and some with a 1-speed.

The incredible thing about biking California style is that you can ride nearly all year around. Rainy days don't last; summers in Central Coast California are never that hot nor winters that cold that you can't ride in comfort. Fog is a year-round expectation and a jacket is a must for coast riding.

The result is miles of great bike trails—Steinbeck country, wineries, gardens, fishing wharfs, the Baylands, Point Lobos and Cannery Row. You can see life close up, how it feels as well as how it looks. From the seat of a bike it is quite a view.

① POINT LOBOS: Jewel of a Ride

Point Lobos State Reserve is often called the "crown jewel of the California State Park System." It is easy to see why. Even at a casual glance you become aware that this is a great outdoor museum encompassing some of the finest rock and surf scenery to be found anywhere. Couple this with the richness of its flowers and wildlife and you can see why Point Lobos is a bike rider's favorite.

You can drive to Point Lobos on Highway 1, south of Carmel, pay $1 to drive in, and then unload your bike. Or you can bike from Carmel by following Highway 1 to the Reserve (25 cents per bike rider), a distance of about two miles. (Add this to the Carmel ride; pick up Highway 1 from Carmel Mission.)

The Reserve provides for bike riding on paved roads only. In addition there are about seven miles of hiking trails.

From the seat of a bicycle, Point Lobos is a beauty. The Reserve is open from 9 A.M. to 7 P.M. daily, and has very strict rules. For example, you cannot collect—not rocks, not shells, not anything. There are 20 picnic tables and some restrooms, but development is kept to a minimum. For this reason, a balance of nature exists and plants and animals are allowed to undergo their natural life cycles without the interference of man.

Over 200 species of birds have been identified within the boundaries. At the ranger station you can buy a booklet for 50 cents to help you identify the birds. It is especially helpful to amateur bird watchers. Three common residents—California quail, belted kingfisher and mourning dove—are easily picked out. Be sure to bring along your binoculars.

POINT LOBOS STATE RESERVE

There are 460 different wildflowers to be seen from your bike; a booklet about them is available for 50 cents. The wildflowers are at their colorful best in late spring and you will want to hike the paths by foot—with camera in hand, naturally—to fully appreciate the flowers.

The Reserve officials ask visitors not to feed the wild life, and one ranger ruefully admitted that "the squirrels have never heard about this rule," so they still sit and beg. It is a hard plea to resist.

The paved roadway on which bikers may travel goes from the park entrance past Whaler's Cottage to Cannery Point. From here you can hike by foot to Whaler's Cove. Then pedal back to the main roadway and across Big Meadows, and loop out to Point Lobos. The point extends into Pinnacle Cove, a footpath, with Carmel Bay on one side and the Pacific Ocean on the other. The paved roadway circles back to Sand Hill Cove, through Little Mound Meadow to Hidden Beach and China Cove. Be sure to walk out to the tip of Point Lobos to view Sea Lion Rock and to the point above China Cove to look at Bird Island.

If it is your lucky day, the sun will be shining. Take a jacket anyway, for it is usually brisk even if the sun is out. More likely, it will be foggy.

CARMEL BAY
WHALER'S COVE
SAN FRANCISCO
ENTRANCE
BIG MEADOW
PINNACLE COVE
HEADLAND COVE
POINT LOBOS RESERVE
HIGHWAY 1
POINT LOBOS
SEA LION COVE
PACIFIC OCEAN
CHINA COVE
BIRD IS.

(2)

CARMEL: Mission Tour

Rugged, sweeping beaches. Stunted cypress reaching against the cold fog. Beautiful little shops. Quaint quiet restaurants. This is Carmel! You can spend a whole week in Carmel and never see a bike rider. But on the weekend, bikers turn out en masse to maneuver the crowded streets of this famous town by the sea.

There is a good reason for the popularity of bicycles in Carmel. Automobile parking is at a premium and traffic snarls are a regular thing, so some visitors find it advantageous to tote along a bike, park a distance from the downtown area, and then pedal around.

Carmel Beach at the foot of Ocean Avenue, the main street of Carmel, is a good spot for home base. There are free parking, restrooms, benches and a pretty beach. For a good three-mile ride from Carmel Beach, go up one street to San Antonio Avenue. Turn right and follow the signs to Carmel Mission. The roadway cuts through an umbrella of cypress trees to Santa Lucia Avenue. Turn left onto Santa Lucia and then right onto Rio Avenue to the Mission.

Carmel Mission was founded in 1770 by Padre Junipero Serra, who is buried within its walls. When the Missions began to die out, Carmel Mission fell to ruin. Its restoration has taken place only in the past 30 years.

Today, the mission is open daily from 9:30 A.M. to 5 P.M. and on Sundays from 10:30 A.M. to 5 P.M. At the entrance you can pick up a pamphlet that is a guide to the mission church, museum, cemetery and Munras Memorial. It is a worthwhile tour. The mission is of Moorish design graced by four bells. Inside the mission, candles flicker, softly sweeping to light the catenary arch of the ceiling. You can spend two hours touring the mission and museum, viewing the picturesque pieces of California's past.

Now bike back Rio Avenue to San Carlos Avenue. Turn right onto San Carlos, which leads to downtown Carmel. Spend the rest of the day biking, browsing in the shops, and enjoying the restaurants for which Carmel is famous. There are a number of galleries, such as Carmel Sculpture at Bell Tower Court and Gallery Mack at Paseo Court, where you will see bright graphics. Works on rice paper by Carmel artist Doris Klumb are on view at her gallery, at the corner of San Carlos and Seventh Street. For something different visit the Brass Rubbing Center, Mission at Eighth Street, where you can make your own brass rubbing in the upstairs studio. Plant lovers, meanwhile, will be enticed by Plantasia in Bell Tower Court. Antiques, books, art galleries, specialty shops—Carmel is an explorer's paradise.

A camera and a jacket both are most necessary. You might be lucky and hit a sunny day, but don't count on it.

Carmel Mission

Statue - Carmel Mission

Carmel Beach

Carmel Mission

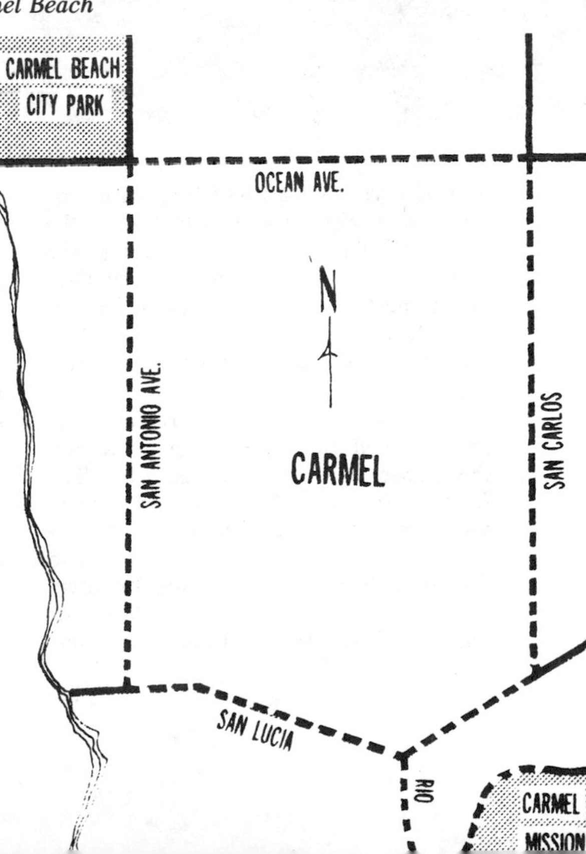

(3) 17-MILE DRIVE: Bike Rider's View

The glorious 17-Mile Drive—the words conjure up visions of ocean surf pounding against sculptured rocks, sand dunes frosted with ice plants, groves of cypress clinging to the cliffs. From a bike you can get your best views of this stunning coast, for you can smell the mist, feel the fog, hear the surf, and see the birds.

You can ride the 17-Mile Drive only on weekdays. It is closed to bikers on weekends and holidays. There is no charge to ride the route. You can enter at any of the toll gates and make the complete round, but the best version starts at the Carmel Hill Gate off Highway 1 on the south end. The gatekeeper

will give you a map which explains the sights and will direct you to "follow the red line." This will take you up to the crest of the ridge to Huckleberry Hill, the highest point in Del Monte Forest, and then wind down past marvelous homes to the water's edge at Spanish Bay.

Along the coast here the route is flat and the pedaling easy. Stop to explore the dunes and wade in the surf. The Restless Sea is off Point Joe, and you can see where several conflicting ocean currents meet, fight with each other, and then beat themselves into foamy breakers against the rocks of Point Joe. You ride past Spyglass Hill Golf Course and then, past Fanshell Beach, begin a gradual climb through Cypress Point Golf Course where bent cypress arch the road. Ride out to Cypress Point Lookout for a smashing view of the rocky coast. On a clear day you can see as far as Big Sur Lighthouse. Lone Cypress, California's most famous landmark, is along here, and you can use a footpath to walk out to the point.

The route now dips down to Del Monte Lodge and Golf Course, headquarters of the Bing Crosby Pro-Am Golf Tournament. (The ride is also closed to bikes during the week of the Pro-Am.) You can explore the Pebble Beach shops and watch the golfers on the easily-recognized 18th hole of the Pebble Beach Course. The road takes you around past the Carmel Gate and uphill to the Highway 1 gate, your starting point.

Another version of the 17-Mile Drive is a mini-ride that still totals 17 miles but eliminates the difficult hill-climbing portion. The mini-ride is recommended for less experienced riders since it does take in the best sights but on an easier pedal. For this ride, start at the Carmel Gate off Ocean Avenue in Carmel. Reverse the numbers on the map, starting with Del Monte Lodge and working your way as far north as Spanish Bay. This is a total of 8½ miles with just enough hill climbing to tease you. At Spanish Bay you can reverse yourself and do the 17-mile out-and-back ride with a rewarding view going in both directions. As you pedal along watch for the wild life such as deer on the golf course, and sea lions and sea otters in the waters and on the rocks offshore. At some places the road and the beach and the view are yours alone; at other places you will be sharing with tourists, photographers and artists.

Either way—loop route or mini-version—you have pedaled 17 miles of singular beauty.

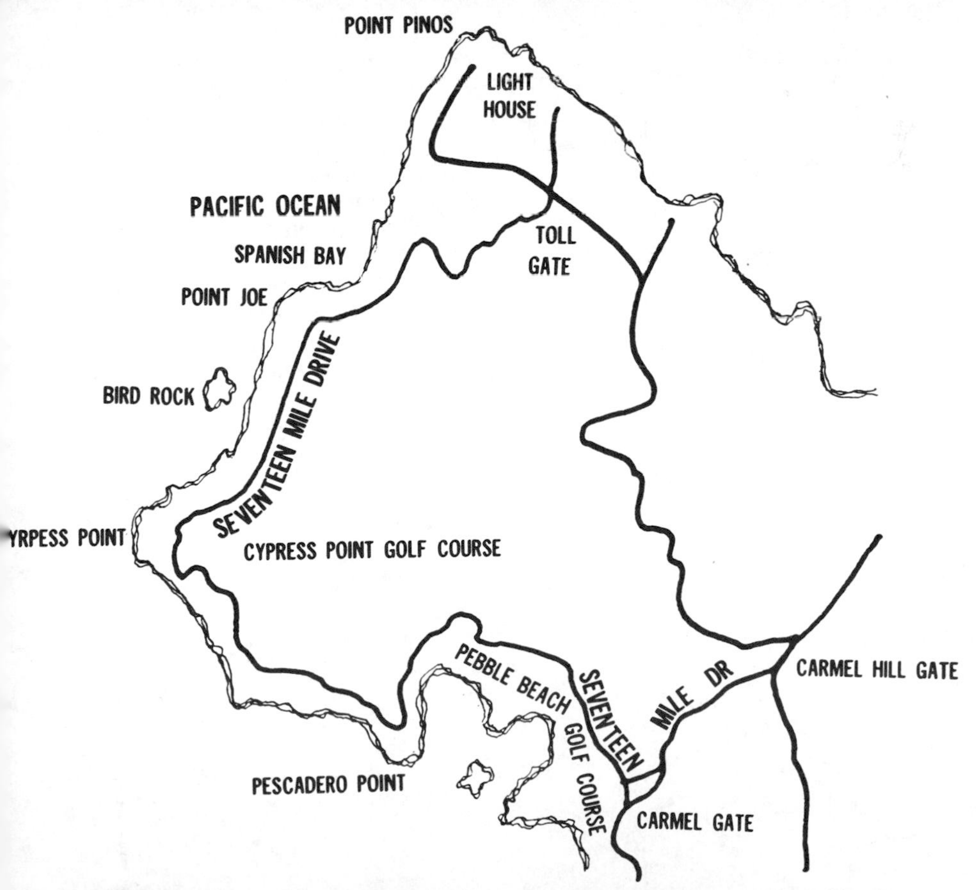
POINT PINOS
LIGHT HOUSE
PACIFIC OCEAN
SPANISH BAY
TOLL GATE
POINT JOE
SEVENTEEN MILE DRIVE
BIRD ROCK
YRPESS POINT
CYPRESS POINT GOLF COURSE
PEBBLE BEACH GOLF COURSE
SEVENTEEN MILE DR
CARMEL HILL GATE
PESCADERO POINT
CARMEL GATE

RIDGE ROUTE: No Stoplights in Sight

A secret route from Carmel to Pacific Grove without traffic or stoplights to slow you down seems hard to believe in this tourist-popular locale. But Highway 68 along the ridge of Del Monte Forest is just that—and in a record eight miles. This can be a one-way or an out-and-back ride because nowhere along here is the ridge route terribly hilly in either direction.

Start at Highway 1 (south) where the sign indicates the 17-Mile Drive-Pacific Grove turnoff. Instead of turning toward 17-Mile Drive, go straight onto Highway 68, also called the W.R. Holman Highway. The wide shoulder serves as a bike path, the uphill pedal is gradual and the turns are well-banked. All along here on the right is a panoramic view of the sandy curve of Monterey Bay to the Santa Cruz Mountains. As the cypress and pine clear on the left, you get a sweeping view of the 17-Mile Drive coastline from Pacific Grove to Point Lobos.

From the highest point in the forest, Huckleberry Hill, the road begins a controlled decline into Pacific Grove, becoming Forest Avenue. Watch for the signs indicating Highway 68, directing you left onto Sunset Drive. Cross over 17-Mile Drive and pedal down to Asilomar Beach State Park. Sea gulls perch on the rocks in the water and sand dunes stand like giant stepping stones. The wave action is incredible, and any place you stop along here you can watch for hours in fascination as breakers crash over rocks, tossing mist high into the air. Like most of the beaches along the coast, this is hazardous water area—for looking, but not swimming.

At the deep point which is Point Pinos, you can pedal out to the spot where Monterey Bay begins. The first right turn is Asilomar Avenue; use this route to ride down to Point Pinos Lighthouse, open Saturday and Sunday from 1 to 4 P.M.

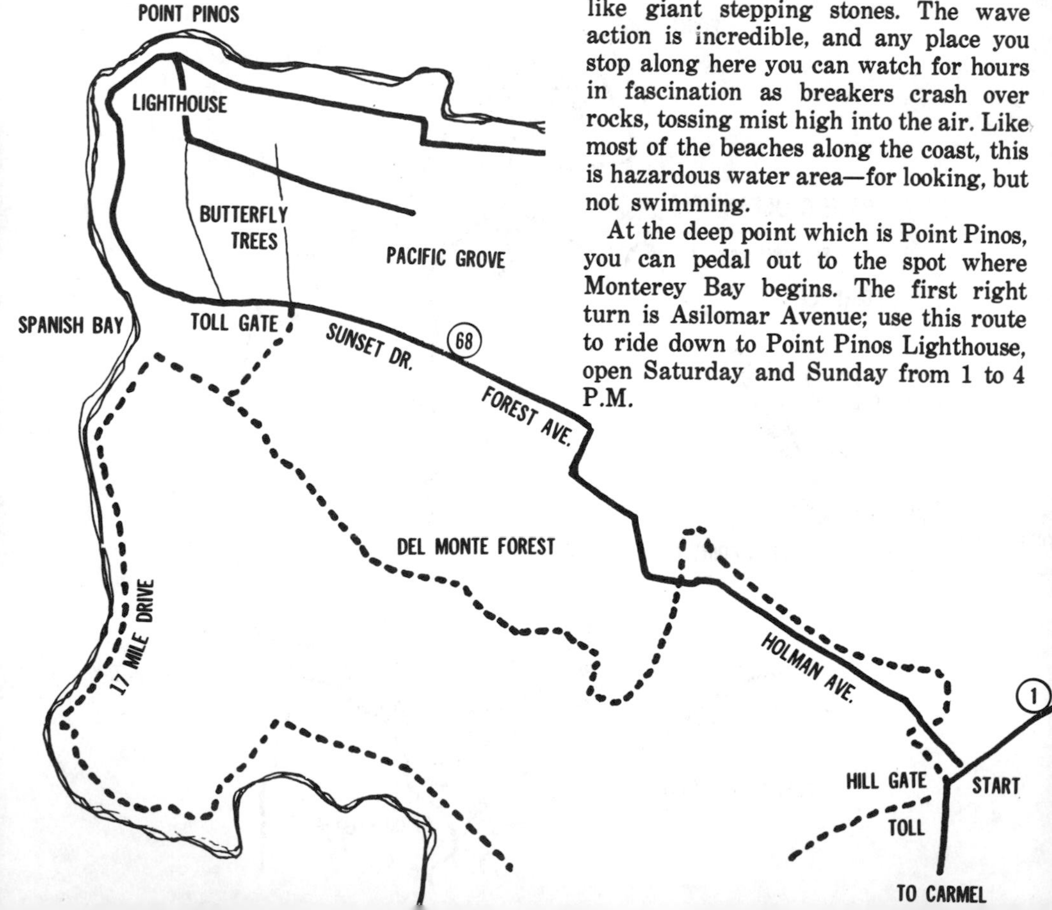

Continue along Asilomar Avenue and turn left onto Lighthouse Avenue. All along here you will see signs of Pacific Grove's own special fall colors—the brilliant orange of the Monarch butterflies. If you pedal this path from October to March, you will see the Monarchs clinging to pine trees along here, or, on a sunny day, swarming around. On the right is Butterfly Lodge and further along is Milar's Butterfly Grove Motel. Both have good groves of Monarchs and welcome visitors to watch, walk and take photographs. Booklets about the Monarchs are also available.

To pedal back to Highway 68, ride Lighthouse Boulevard until it crosses 17-Mile Drive, turn right on the drive and pick up Holman Highway for the return trip across the Del Monte Forest ridge.

⑤ PACIFIC GROVE: From End to End

Pacific Grove, from one end to the other, is best seen from the seat of a bicycle. If it is sunny and warm, that's a bonus. But foggy and cool weather (always take a jacket when biking the Monterey Peninsula) gives an entirely different perspective to this world-famous stretch of coast that you can explore in a six-mile loop.

Start from Point Pinos Lighthouse on Asilomar Avenue at the tip of Pacific Grove. The lighthouse is open to visitors on Saturday and Sunday from 1 to 4 P.M. Pedal left onto Asilomar Avenue, and then turn right onto Ocean View Boulevard. The scenery is spectacular and all along here the road is flanked on the ocean side by a beautifully landscaped garden which is called the Grove Marine Gardens Park. Stop at Lovers Point to see the scuba divers practicing their skills in the cove. There are glass bottom boats, a marine garden and, in summer, a municipal pool located here. The attractive Victorian building overlooking the cove is the Old Bath House, now converted to a gourmet restaurant.

Ocean View Boulevard gives way to the boat works as you enter Monterey. The first left turn is David Avenue and this takes you downhill to Cannery Row. Shops and boutiques of every description line the street, with antiques and arts and crafts the primary offerings. The eating places are among the best known on the Monterey Peninsula, and casually dressed bikers are welcome for lunch anywhere.

As you pedal out the far end of Cannery Row, bike up two blocks on Drake Avenue and turn right onto Lighthouse Avenue. After three blocks turn left onto David Avenue to pick up residential Lighthouse Avenue for a leisurely ride back to Pacific Grove. Along here are some great old Victorian homes—Pacific Grove has a thing about restoring them—and there is a full block of restored Victorian shops near Grand Avenue in downtown Pacific Grove. The Pacific Grove Museum of Natural History and the Art Center are on the right at Forest Avenue and both are open to the public without cost Tuesday through Sunday.

After crossing 17-Mile Drive, watch for signs indicating the Monarch Butterfly Trees. The Monarchs spend every winter clustered on the pine trees here and the butterflies can be seen on clear days from October to March. Many of them are on trees at Milar's Grove on the left side of Lighthouse Avenue, some can be seen along Butterfly Lane, and many more can be seen at Butterfly Lodge on the right.

At Asilomar Avenue, turn right to return to the starting point at the lighthouse.

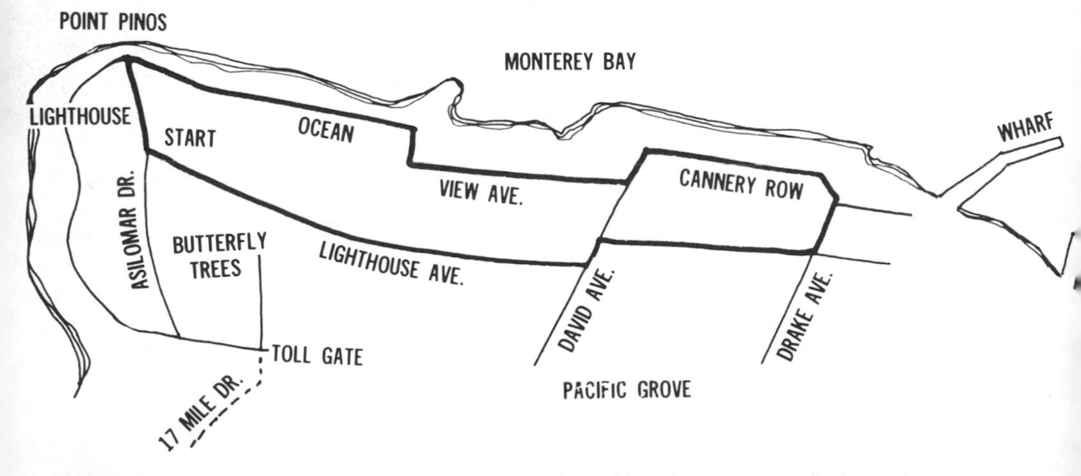

Butterfly Grove

Point Pinos

Asilomar Beach

6 MONTEREY: Path of History

Monterey is a delightful city which has chosen to preserve that which is old and beautiful and very much California. The Monterey Path of History is a natural for bike riders; three miles of nicely marked route pass by massive old adobe structures, most of which are open to the public.

A camera and a jacket are musts. Chilly fog is more the rule than the exception on the Monterey Peninsula and it can be unpleasantly cold without a coverup, even in summer.

The Path of History starts at the First French Consulate, located on Camino El Ester, and finishes near the same spot. You can park your car here, unload your bike and pedal away. There are 45 locations marked along the Path showing where much of California's early history took place. Some are National Historical Landmarks, some are State Historical Landmarks, and some are private buildings not open to the public.

Popular spots include California's first theater, the Royal Presidio Chapel, the Casa Del Oro House and the Robert Louis Stevenson House, which is open from 9 A.M. to 5 P.M. At the Custom House overlooking Fisherman's Wharf, park your bike and walk out on the wharf. Sample the terrific eating places, both good and inexpensive, and watch the fishing boats dock.

From the wharf, pedal a side trip to nearby Cannery Row (follow the signs) for a closeup view of the sardine canneries made famous by writer John Steinbeck. The old canneries still stand, but art galleries, studios, antique shops and import shops share the premises with restaurants. There is nary a sardine in sight.

A copy of the Path of History map is available by writing the Monterey Peninsula Chamber of Commerce, P.O. Box 1770, Monterey, CA 93940. Or just follow the route, which is plainly marked with a red guide line down the center of the street and Path of History signs along the way. Each of the 45 sites bears a marker which tells that page of history.

If California history is your particular interest, and especially if you have grade school youngsters studying California, this is a winning ride.

Cannery Row

600
FIGUEROA ST.
PATH OF HISTORY

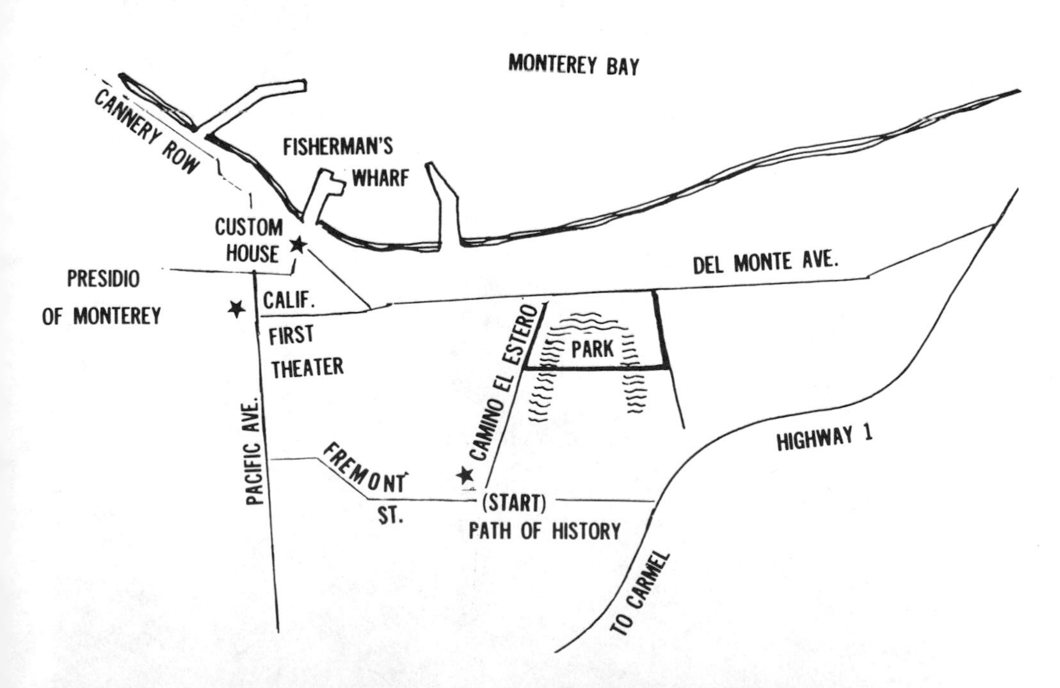
MONTEREY BAY
CANNERY ROW
FISHERMAN'S
WHARF
CUSTOM
HOUSE
PRESIDIO
OF MONTEREY
CALIF.
FIRST
THEATER
DEL MONTE AVE.
PARK
CAMINO EL ESTERO
PACIFIC AVE.
FREMONT
ST.
(START)
PATH OF HISTORY
HIGHWAY 1
TO CARMEL

(7)

PRESIDIO TO FORT ORD: Army-Navy Game

Think about things military on the Monterey Peninsula and your mind will center on the Presidio of Monterey, the U.S. Naval Postgraduate School, and Fort Ord. You can see two of these and also include a nautical visit to Monterey Fisherman's Wharf in a ten-mile loop route, or see all three by going on to Fort Ord for a one-way 15-mile ride.

To start, drive into the Presidio Main Gate on Artillery Drive and park at the U.S. Army Museum. Open from 9 to 12:30 and 1:30 to 4 daily except Tuesday and Wednesday, the museum tells about the Presidio, which was founded in 1770 and fell into U.S. hands when Commodore John Drake Sloan captured Monterey on July 7, 1846. From the museum, bike around the Presidio, bearing always to the right, and circle around the Sports Arena to the Memorial Statue commemorating Sloan. This is one of the highest spots in Monterey and from here you can see across the bay to Santa Cruz and understand the commanding power that cannons mounted on the hill once had. From the statue you can explore the Presidio grounds, following roads that circle the center Green.

Bike out the main gate at Artillery Drive and turn right onto Pacific Street to work your way down to Fisherman's Wharf. On the wharf you will find restaurants and shops, plus hungry sea gulls waiting for the fishermen to unload their catches and share some scraps.

Now pedal along the waterfront and turn left onto Del Monte Avenue. Be sure to detour through El Estero Park, circling around to pedal across the white bridges. Dennis the Menace Playground is here and so is a lovely lake with shore birds and ducks, and boats for hire.

Back on Del Monte continue to the U.S. Naval Postgraduate School. Inside the main gate is a large map explaining the layout of this park-like campus for the language institute. Pick a path and pedal around. You can circle all around the buildings and trees past a little lake. Keep in mind that you want to come out the same gate you entered, for your return ride to the Presidio.

If a long distance—and more of the military—is your goal, you can continue on Del Monte toward Fort Ord. This is a tricky path and it is best to use a city map. Del Monte will take you north past Sand City to merge with Fremont Street in Seaside. At this point, Fremont loops under the freeway to join Highway 1. Watch for the sign indicating "bike path." From here a paved bike path follows the curve of sand dunes on the ocean side of Ford Ord past the rifle ranges. The paved route concludes along Highway 1 at the 12th Street Gate of the Army Training Center. Visitors are welcome to Fort Ord, but you must go through a sign-in procedure and check to gain entry to the main garrison.

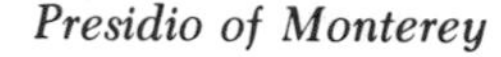

Presidio of Monterey

Presidio - Army Museum

Pond - El Estero Park

U.S. Navy Postgraduate School

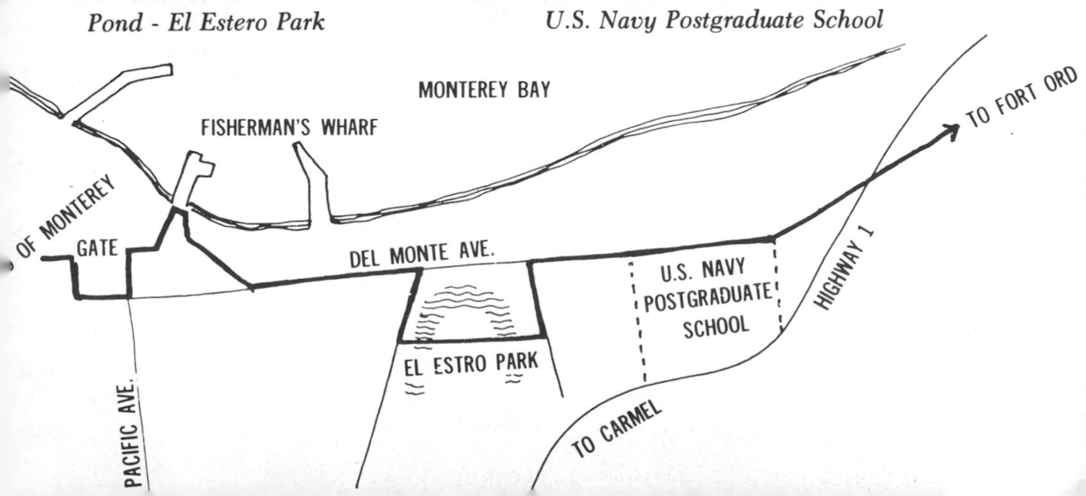

⑧ MONTEREY-SALINAS: Toro Park

A hill that doesn't really "feel" like a strenuous hill-climbing challenge is the ride from Monterey Bay to Salinas Valley by way of Highway 68, the Monterey-Salinas Road. No mistake—it is a hill, strictly speaking. But the inclines are so gradual that the uphill portion is not difficult for 10-speed bikers. It is a good ride for those just getting the feel of long distance riding.

For the ten-mile one-way route, start from Highway 1 at Sand City Beach where the Holiday Inn is the only building on the beach. From Sand Dune Road, ride on Canyon del Rey Boulevard toward the hills through the city of Del Rey Oaks. The rural part of Canyon del Rey is the steepest part of the ride, but the road soon merges with Highway 68.

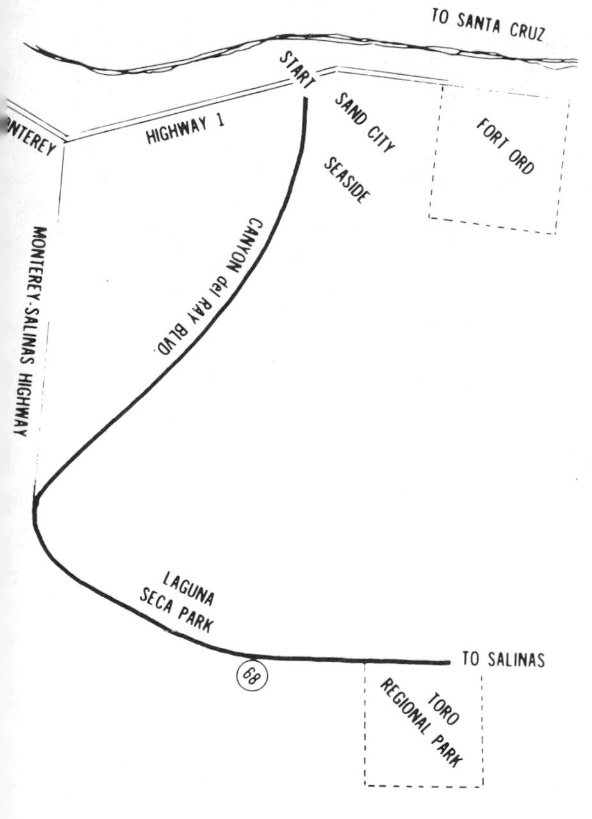

The Monterey-Salinas Road has a wide shoulder to serve as a bike path. On the Monterey side of the coastal hill the road edges Laguna Seca Golf Course and Laguna Seca Raceway, all the while working gradually upward. The hillside is green and pretty with oaks and boulders and ranches scattered around. The weather becomes noticeably warmer as you move away from the ocean and positively hot in summer as you cross the summit and drop into the Salinas Valley side of the hill.

The downhill portion is a quick descent into the farmland of Steinbeck country with a vast patchwork of farms stretching across the Long Valley. Watch for the brick entrance to Toro Regional Park on the right as you come down to the flatland. The park is open from 8 A.M. to dusk and you pay a use fee of 50 cents. There are both bike trails and horse trails, but the park is best known for its hiking trails. There are seven in all, including a 2.7-mile one that climbs to Eagle Rock for a view in one direction of Monterey Bay, from where you have just biked, and Salinas Valley in the other direction. The park is five miles from Salinas, but Highway 68 becomes freeway past the park and you cannot use it for biking.

You can picnic at the park; there are breezy open spaces ideal for kite flying, and a good playground. You have the choice of making this a one-way ride or pedaling back another ten miles. The return ride is an equally good, strenuous trip with some tough ascents.

Sand City Beach

Below: Toro Regional Park

9

SALINAS: Steinbeck Country

Steinbeck Country starts in Salinas. By bike you can sample a bit of that flavor of John Steinbeck's home town, for the city pridefully retains that touch. The natural backdrop of Steinbeck Country—fields, rivers, forests and mountains—is as visual now as when the author described it. The Red Pony still roams the Long Valley. Lettuce is still Salinas Valley's "green gold." Buckeyes still bloom in the springtime in the Pastures of Heaven.

You can see it all close-up by bike. Start your bike ride at the Steinbeck House, 132 Central Avenue. This was the birthplace of Steinbeck in 1902 and has been described in *East of Eden*, a chronicle of life in Salinas Valley at the turn of the century.

The great old Victorian house has been redecorated inside and out. Now it serves as a luncheon tea room owned and operated by Valley Guild, with profits going toward the renovation of Steinbeck House and to charities. Lunch is served in the parlor Monday through Friday at 11:45 and at 1:15. Advance reservations are needed.

con't

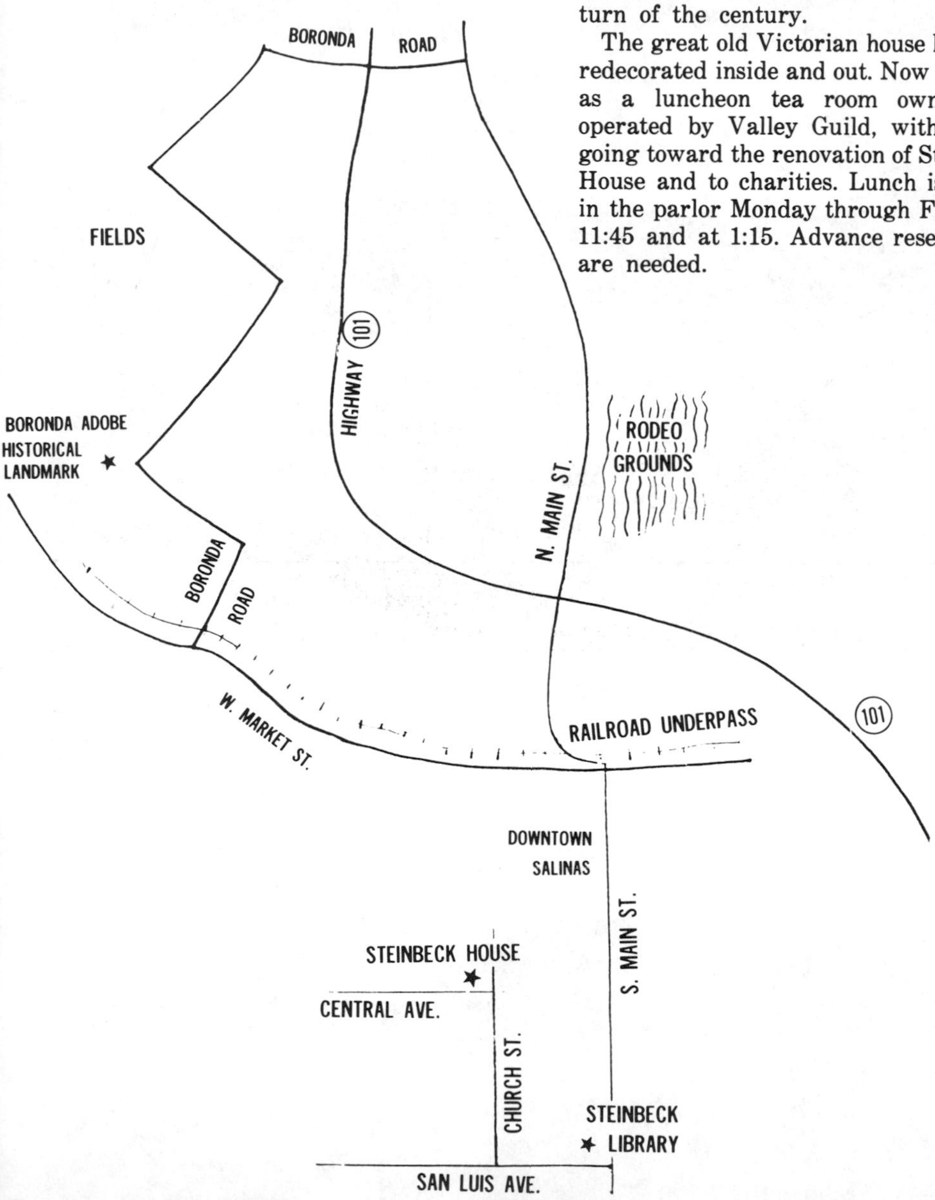

Above: Steinbeck Library
Upper: John Steinbeck's birthplace
Left: Steinbeck Statue outside John Steinbeck Library

Adobe along Steinbeck Trail

From Steinbeck House, pedal down Church Street to the Steinbeck Library, 110 West San Luis Avenue. Steinbeck did much research for *East of Eden* here. There is a Steinbeck Room with photographs, memorabilia, first editions and original manuscripts. This entire library is an unusual place, with a sunny patio-reading room and another reading room with great bean bag pillows on the floor for sprawling out with a favorite book.

Now bike back down to South Main Street. This is the "original square mile" of Salinas, which is being revitalized. Steinbeck's father, J. Ernst Steinbeck Sr., was a hay and grain merchant here.

Ride on South Main Street through the railroad underpass. Continue on this street (which becomes North Main St.) to the Salinas Rodeo Grounds. Sherwood Park, with a swimming pool and picnic area, is adjacent to the Rodeo Grounds. From here you can go in any direction to explore Steinbeck Country, for the fields of lettuce and strawberries stretch out in every direction.

One view of the great open country: go down North Main Street, turn left onto Boronda Street and then pedal past the fields of strawberries and lettuce where workers are busy picking the crops or tending the plants. Boronda eventually works its way back to West Market Street; turn left to pedal back to downtown Salinas.

The Salinas Chamber of Commerce publishes a Steinbeck Country brochure for 50 cents which outlines four one-day self-guided tours which range in length from 55 to 115 miles. For the long-distance touring cyclists—and especially Steinbeck buffs—the booklet is worth having, for it spotlights the areas in the Monterey Peninsula that Steinbeck used as settings for his novels. For copies, write Salinas Chamber of Commerce, 119 East Alisal Avenue, Salinas, CA 93901.

Annual scene at great rodeo
Picking strawberries

San Juan Bautista is the City of History "...where the charm of the past lingers into the present." Bicycling is a delightful way to view close up that combination of past and present.

San Juan Bautista is located three miles off Highway 101. It is a quiet little town surrounded by pretty green rolling hills and cattle ranches. You can pedal around the entire area very easily, which makes it an ideal bike ride for even the youngest rider. Weekdays there is little traffic; on the weekends a bike is perfect for wiggling in and out of tourist traffic.

Many of the shops and restaurants are located in historic buildings over 100 years old. There are antique shops, specialty shops, restaurants, and a fantastic little bakery that's right out of the 20s. Galleries show works of local artists and craftsmen, as well as those from other parts of California. You can watch the potter, the painter, or the candlestick maker at his craft.

The charm of San Juan is that the city fathers have chosen to preserve what is old and beautiful. Down Second Street are the first houses built by emigrant families. Some of the oldest residents of San Juan were survivors of the Donner Party. Main Street is lined with the old shops. One is the DeAnza House, which stands as it did in 1799. The adobe walls and beamed ceiling are exposed inside, and the building now houses an antique shop with a residence in back.

The focal point of San Juan is the plaza, where the famed Mission San Juan Bautista was founded in 1797. In design the church is the largest in the state's

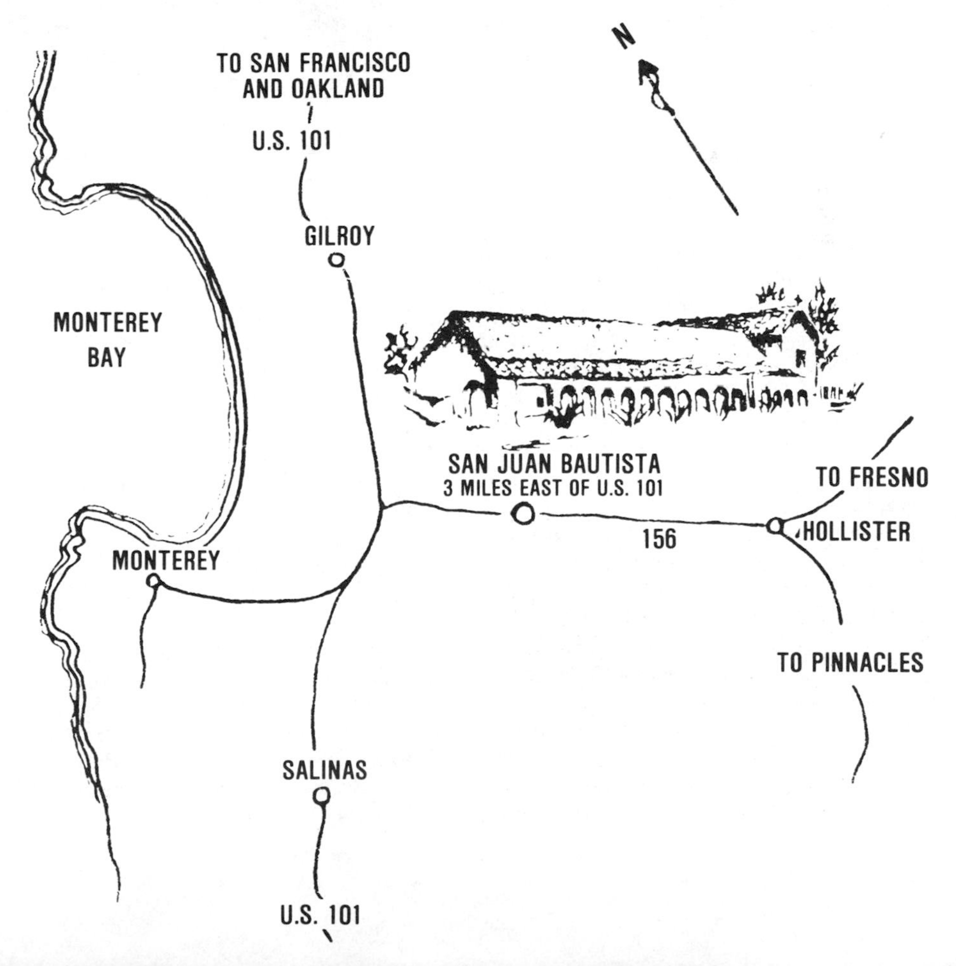

Mission San Juan Bautista

mission chain and faces one of the few remaining original Spanish plazas. The mission is open daily to visitors at no charge. To the right of the mission entrance is a slope that appears to drop down to the valley below. It is really the San Andreas Fault, for the mission padres built just a few feet from the fault. Yet they built so well that their mission still stands, after 275 years of shakes and tremors.

History buffs will love to bike across the plaza to the State Historic Park. Numerous buildings—Castro Adobe, Plaza Hall, the jail and a log cabin—are open for public inspection. One of the prettiest spots is the garden behind the Plaza Hotel. It is beautifully tended with flowers and cactus all summer long.

You can pick up a brochure at the State Park Office in the Plaza. Better yet, buy a copy of the booklet "A Walking Guide to San Juan Bautista" and adapt it to biking. If you follow the text of the book, it will take you from the earliest buildings in San Juan to the later ones and help you understand some of the dramatic moments in history that lie behind the quiet scenery of today.

Using the guide as your map, a sightseeing bike ride including th mission and the buildings of the state historic park, and browsing in a few shops, can be accomplished in three hours—unless you get hooked on the shops. Then you could spend the weekend.

For a longer ride, you can go out of town on Second Street and loop around the mission to the San Juan Valley below. Long distance riders can travel the Salinas Grade. This is the old Highway 101 to Salinas, and as its name suggests, it has its "ups and downs."

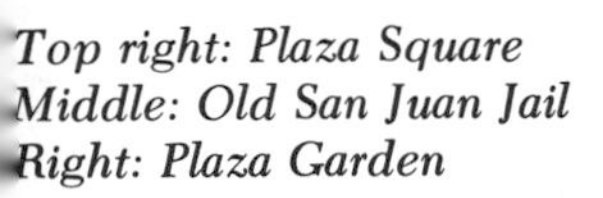

Top right: Plaza Square
Middle: Old San Juan Jail
Right: Plaza Garden

MOSS LANDING: Short Hill Hops

Moss Landing is popular with bikers both as the destination point for long distance touring clubs and as a short hop for the "Sunday biker." There are two good bike routes which begin from Moss Landing Marina, one that loops south through Castroville, and another that circles north onto San Miguel Canyon Road.

The ten-mile ride through Castroville is suited even for beginning riders, for it follows gently rolling hills and flat artichoke country. Pedal up Dolan Road, which bisects the PG&E and Kaiser plants on Highway 1. Cows and artichoke fields are the main interest along here. The uphill pedal is so gradual you are hardly aware of it. Turn right onto Castroville Road for a steeper climb that drops down to the town of Castroville. Bear to the right on Highway 1, skimming the freeway to turn onto the main street of Castroville. At the intersection is The Great Artichoke, a fruit and vegetable stand and restaurant. This is the place to sample artichokes—boiled, fried or stuffed—or you can buy a root to grow your own, or dried artichoke puffs for flower arrangements.

Pedal through downtown Castroville under the arch that proclaims the town the "Artichoke Center of the World." There are a number of eating places and shops worth investigating. Merritt Avenue becomes Highway 1 outside of town, where you are once again surrounded by fields of the artichokes which grow so well on this cool foggy coast.

As you approach Moss Landing, veer to the left onto Moss Landing Road past the cemetery. You will pass some neat antique shops, an old book store, and fish and tackle shops. Turn left onto Sandholt Road to cross the bridge back to the Marina.

Another version of this route leads up to the hill area through clumps of oak, madrone and maple trees. As you ride up Dolan Road, turn left onto Castroville Road. This section has the longest climb on the loop, a little over one mile, but the grade is slight. A sharp descent takes you down to San Miguel Road, which is well traveled but also has a good shoulder for biking. Turn left onto Hall Road and cross the valley onto Elkhorn Road. Elkhorn is a nice bike-riding road that climbs a half-mile to a ridge above the slough. Watch for birds. The redwing blackbird will be the easiest to spot, but the area around Elkhorn Slough is famous for its varied bird population so take along a pair of binoculars and see how many you can find.

Elkhorn Road is a very lightly traveled country road that twists and turns through eucalyptus along the slough. The route brings you back around to Dolan Road and you can pedal back to the Marina, a distance of 14 miles.

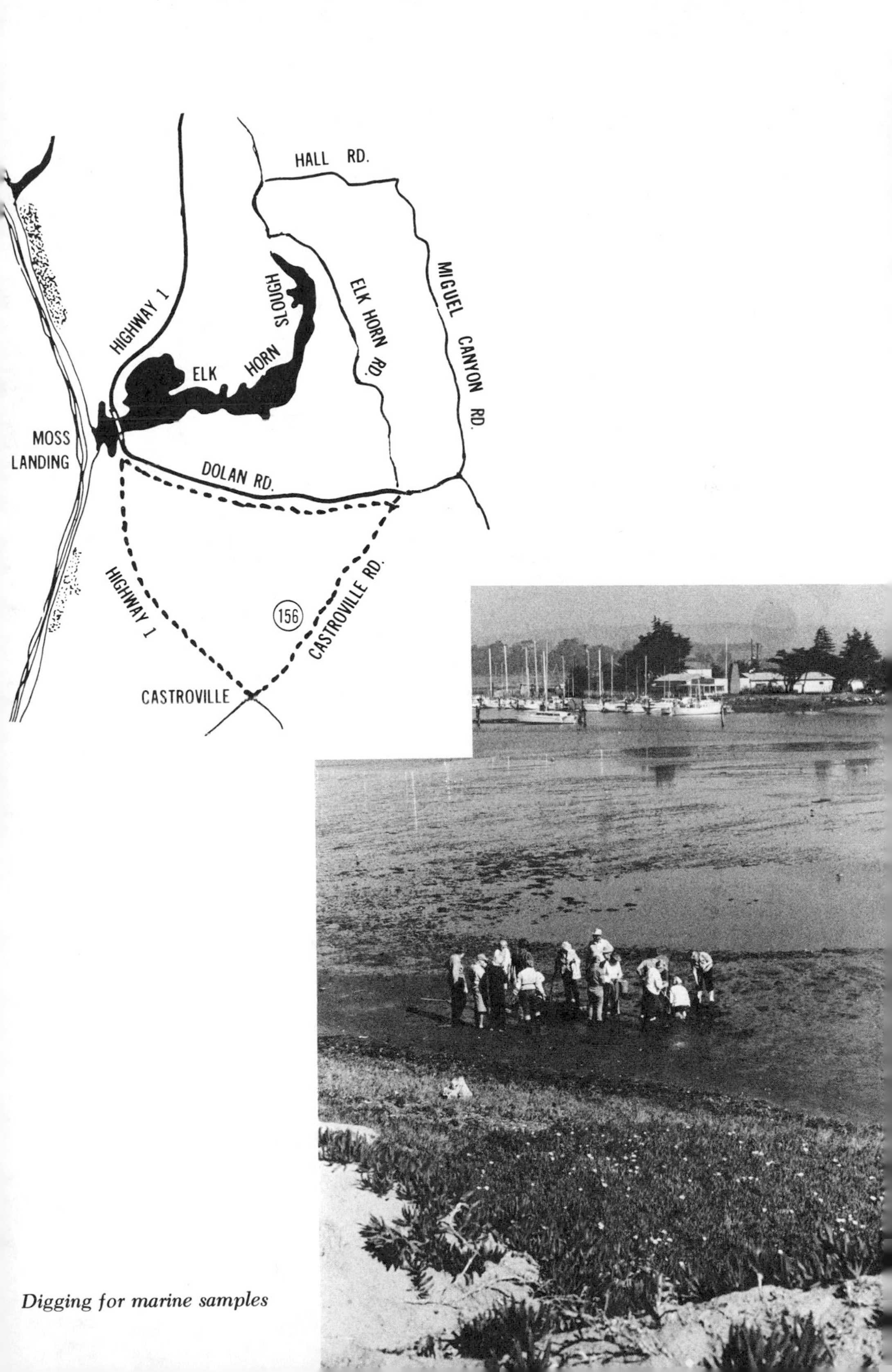

Digging for marine samples

MOSS LANDING: Beach Combers

Sand dunes, waves pounding the Moss Landing breakwater, fields of artichokes and vegetables extending from the edge of the beach to the foothills—this is the setting for an easy pedal on the beaches of Moss Landing. The Monterey Bay dominates the terrain, and all roads lead to the water's edge.

Start from Moss Landing Marina, where sailboats and yachts are moored alongside fishing boats. Pedal from the Marina and turn left onto Cabrillo Highway (Highway 1), riding north toward the Salinas Road intersection. Turn left onto Stuve Road where the sign indicates Zmundowski Beach State Park. The road weaves back and forth through patchwork parcels of farmland, past the Pajaro River Slough to the sand dune-lined beach. The dunes along here are especially popular with horseback riders. You can park your bike anywhere along the long, lonely beach and walk in the surf, picking up sand dollars and tiny shells. On a weekday you may have the beach all to yourself; on weekends, others will share your pleasure.

Now pedal back out to Cabrillo Highway and ride past the Yacht Club to Jetty Road to reach Moss Landing State Beach. This is a popular spot with surf fishermen, and you can ride out to the tip of the rocky breakwater for a terrific view of Moss Landing's coast. The boats are moored in the marina; the PG&E hydro-electric plant looms behind you; on a clear day you can see all the way around the bay from Point Pinos to the south to Santa Cruz to the north. Signs along here warn of riptides and dangerous water, yet you will see some surfers in wetsuits riding the breakers. You can rent a pole and buy bait at a number of shops by the water and try for a catch of perch or rock cod off the breakwater.

Cabrillo Highway takes you south where antique shops, fishing tackle and bait shops, and a couple of stores make

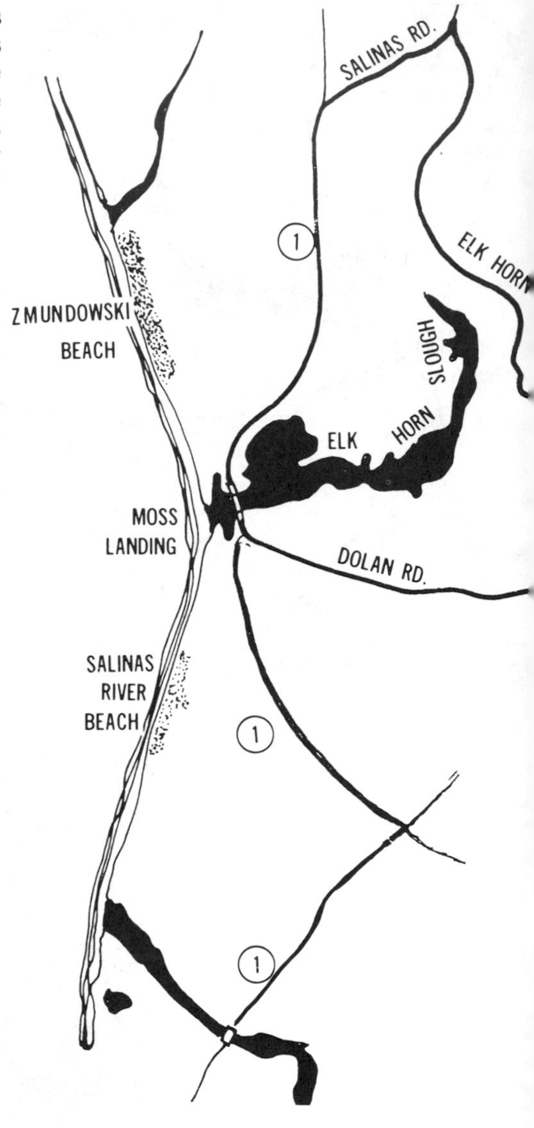

up the town of Moss Landing. Across the bridge on the "island" are the boat works and commercial fishing interests. Also located here and open to visitors on weekdays is Moss Landing Marine Laborator-

con't

Above: Moss Landing breakwater

Zmundowski Beach sand dunes

ies of the California Colleges and Universities. You can walk into the buildings and look around, as long as you remember that there are outdoor classes and research going on. The focus of all the attention at the Marine Laboratories is the Monterey Submarine Canyon, a gold mine of deep water research that begins where Elkhorn Slough empties into the bay at Moss Landing. Along the beach, tide pools turn up interesting samples and toward Elkhorn Slough, bird and marsh study is being done. Using a wild life handbook as a guide, you can spot from your bike many of the things that have brought the students to Moss Landing.

As you cross back from the "island," continue on Moss Landing Road past the cemetery and turn right to pedal out to Salinas River State Beach. More sand dunes and a stretch of very pretty and secluded beach await you here. You can ride the same road back to the Marina for a total of eight miles.

SAN JUAN GRADE: Over the Gabilans

A terrific bike trail cuts right up the eastern slope of the Gabilan Mountains, through San Juan Pass to Salinas Valley for ten miles of good mountain climbing. Make no mistake, the Salinas Road-San Juan Grade (the name changes at the crest) is a tough uphill challenge. It is definitely a 10-speed bike ride; the inclines start easy and if you know how to use your gears you can ride it with pleasure.

Start at the Plaza at San Juan Bautista Mission, where you can first explore some of the historic old buildings which have been beautifully preserved. From the Plaza take Washington Street and turn left onto Third Street to pedal out of town. Cross Highway 156 at the stop light; Third Street becomes Salinas Road across the highway. Keep to the right as the well-patched worn county road begins to wind upward through the ranch land.

Along here are the rolling hills and clumps of oak and madrone, plus cattle on range land that has changed little since the longhorns were brought to the rancheros here from Northern Mexico. After you climb the first hill you will pedal past a Charolais cattle ranch. An attractive white frame house that is set off by neat white board fences to mark off the corrals, stables and pastures takes this scene right out of the 1850s. The white cattle are scattered on the hills and only they will notice that you have to get off your bike to walk up the sharp turns.

Even on the hottest days, when the Gabilans have been burned bronze by the summer sun, you can look across to the San Juan Valley below and see the irrigated green fields. At any point on this ride you have a perfect open view of the valley.

Beyond the Charolais cattle ranch the terrain is pure mountain country. A weathered board fence marks the road's edge, the only sign of progress. The incline is steadily upward, but never so sharp that the rider has difficulty. Except for an occasional farm truck, the road is little used so you have the wide road all to yourself upward for most of five miles.

At the pass is a straight stretch of roadway before the downhill sweep into Salinas Valley. This portion of San Juan Grade touches on the old Rancho San Antonio land. As you speed downward—and it is definitely a downhill ride all the way—you pass only one ranch, on the left, with cowboys working the cattle. San Juan Grade comes out on the Salinas Valley side at Crazyhorse Canyon Road. It is another five miles from Crazyhorse to North Main Street at Northridge Shopping Mall.

Be aware if you decide to try this ride from the Salinas side that San Juan Grade ascent is a much steeper ride and noticeably more difficult. If you want a loop ride, travel from San Juan Mission to the pass and then turn around to coast back down. Either looped to the summit or all the way over to Crazyhorse Canyon it is a total distance of ten miles straight up and then straight down.

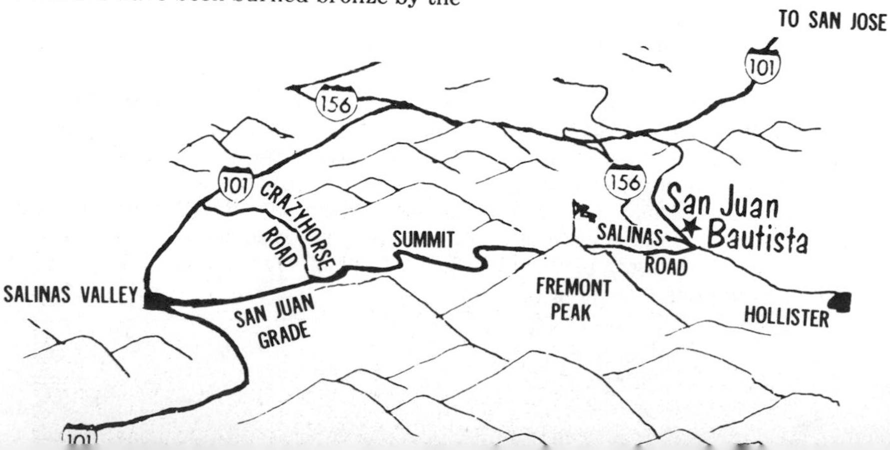

Mission San Juan Bautista

Looking toward San Juan Valley
Salinas Road - San Juan Grade; Charolais Cattle Ranch

⑭ ANDERSON DAM: Wine Country

A bit of the rich agricultural heritage of the south Santa Clara Valley can be seen on a 12-mile south county rural loop. The ride over flat, well-surfaced country roads features a picnic—and fishing—spot, a side trip to Hill Country where free of charge you can view woodcarvings, ancient wagons, old automobiles, and vintage airplanes, plus a cool rest at Filice Winery tasting room. In between, orchards, rows of crops, and livestock punctuate the landscape, bordered all around with oak-etched hills.

Start the ride at Coyote River Park, Anderson Unit, on Cochran Road in Morgan Hill, where parking is available. Barbecue units, picnic tables, tree-shaded walkways, a rushing stream—from Anderson Dam just above—that may yield a fish or two, and a waterfall are here. The park is open, without cost, from 8 A.M. to one-half hour after sunset.

Now use Coyote Road to climb and turn to the face of Anderson Dam. Keep a wary eye out for cars hauling boats on the curves here, for the dam is one of the favorite south county spots for boating and water skiing. Once past the face of the dam, the way is straight and level.

At Main Avenue turn right, continuing to Hill Road where a left turn is indicated. From Hill Road turn left onto Tennant Road, which takes you to Foothill and a side trip to Hill Country.

Bike riders visiting Hill Country will enjoy seeing the two huge hangar-like structures housing collections of old wagons, antique automobiles and airplanes, and unique woodcarvings. Familiar faces, such as those of Will Rogers, Shirley Temple, and the Marx Brothers, peer out from amid the displays. Hill Country is also the site of hot-air balloon racing and if it is your lucky weekend, the colorful great balloons will be soaring overhead. Rides are usually available for a small fee.

Take Foothill back to Tennant Road, turn left, and continue on Condit Road, after a right turn, to the Filice Winery Tasting Room. Even without a few sips of the fine Filice wines, a rest in the shade of the oak trees here is worth the time before continuing on Condit.

On the way to the next right turn, onto Hale Road, you will see the Charro arena where the heritage of the Mexican cowboy is preserved and applauded. Turn left onto Peet Road for an easy ride back to Cochran, where a brief sprint will bring you back to Coyote River Park.

This is a ride that is appealing to young riders because both the distance and the sights along the way are worthy of their interest.

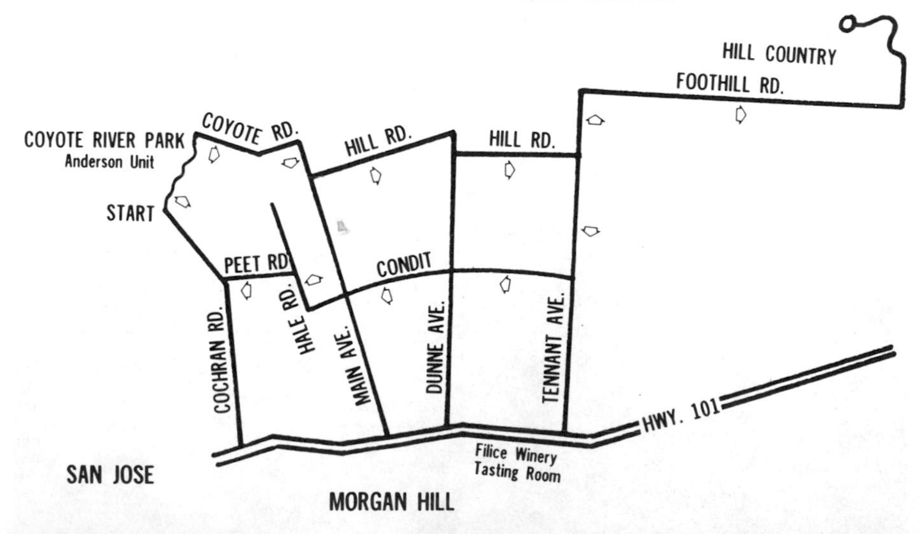

Top: Pastoral scene
Center left: Filice Winery, Gilroy
Middle: Wheeling past old tank house
Right: Shade trees and orchards
Left: Airplane and old automobile museum

CAPITOLA: Sea Tree Tour

Santa Cruz is a natural biking location because you can pedal around the beachside city to your heart's content, exploring the great views and easily marked routes. One example of a good route and pretty view—especially on a sunny day—is from the Boardwalk at Santa Cruz Beach south along East Cliff Drive to Capitola Beach.

This loop ride is part of the Sea Tree Tour called Capitola Loop, and you could simply follow the Capitola Loop sign and do without a map. Or turn off onto some of the side streets to bypass those streets where traffic is heavy, and your reward will be more enjoyable and safer riding. These are *some* hills, but an energetic rider will find the extra effort well worth the rewards.

From Beach Street, start on Riverside Avenue, cross the bridge, turn right onto San Lorenzo Boulevard, and then right onto East Cliff Drive for a leisurely—although sometimes uphill—pace to Santa Cruz Yacht Harbor. Do stop here, since this is one of the most peaceful and picturesque spots in Santa Cruz. It is well worth the time to pedal past the boats moored here and ride out to the breakwater to watch the sailboats fighting the wind and the fishermen casting for perch and cod.

Continue on East Cliff Drive to the Twin Lakes area, a good spot for bikini watchers, and then past the beach houses to Pleasure Point. From here you can watch the surfers in action.

Bear to the right on East Cliff Drive, which becomes Opal Cliff Drive. This is a "bypass" route that loops past beachfront homes and runs back into busy Portola Drive. Ahead is a very beautiful downhill approach to Capitola, a little town tucked away privately in a pretty cove. At Capitola ride onto Esplanada Drive past the wharf and fun center to Monterey Avenue. Be sure to ride out to the pier and explore some of the shops and boutiques in Capitola.

You can return to Santa Cruz Boardwalk by the same route, with only the tough uphill pedal from Capitola to deter you. Better yet, be adventuresome and explore your own route back to Santa Cruz Beach. There is much sea to see. It is 12 miles round trip.

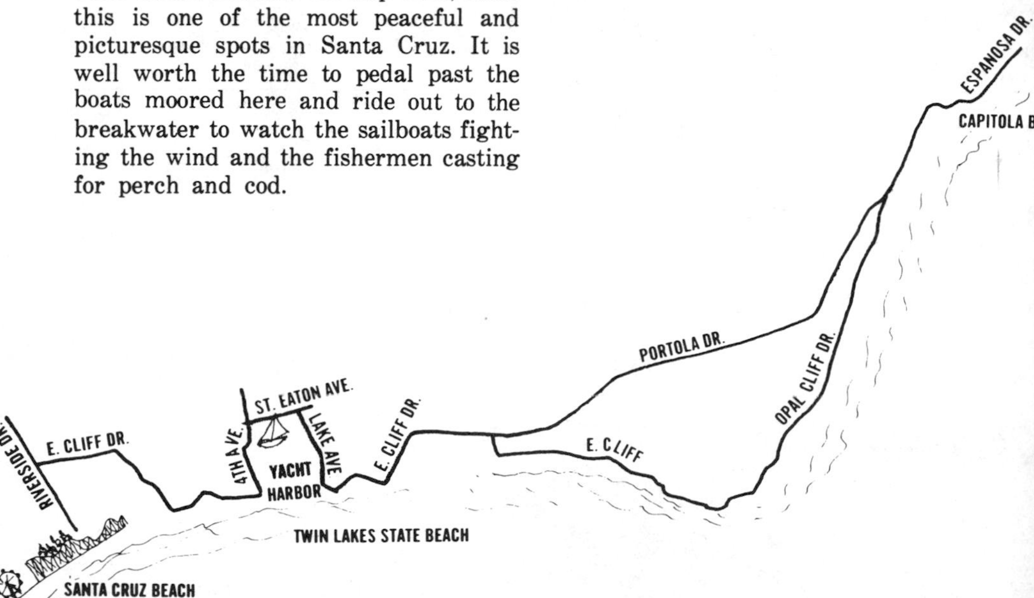

Santa Cruz Boardwalk
Above and below: Santa Cruz Yacht Harbor
Lower left: Capitola

SANTA CRUZ: Cliff Drive

Crashing waves eroding huge cliffs, surfers riding the breakers, sailboats on the horizon—all add up to a bike rider's dream along Santa Cruz's beautiful shoreline.

From the Municipal Pier at the Boardwalk, along West Cliff Drive to Natural Bridges State Beach is some of the most spectacular ocean scenery in the area. If you happen to hit a sunny warm day, consider that a bonus.

The eight miles from the Pier to Natural Bridges is a leisurely-paced ride without even a hint of a hill, which makes this route the best and most scenic of the beginner's rides. Even the youngest rider or first-class novice can go this distance.

At the Pier ride out to the end of the wharf and watch the boats come in with the day's catch. If fishing is your thing, take along a folding fishing rod and drop a line over the side where rock cod and perch will nibble at any bait. There are some terrific restaurants on the Pier, including some with "walk-away" crab cocktails for a snack.

As you come off the Pier, turn left onto West Cliff Drive. Stop at the Light House and ride out to the point for a look through the telescope at the seals on the rocks nearby. Santa Cruz's best surfing waves are along this portion of West Cliff Drive, and any place you stop you are sure to catch the surfers in action, even on the windiest, coldest day. Sailboats also fight the wind around the Light House point. You can sit on a rock and watch it all for five minutes or five hours.

Every turn of the road in West Cliff Drive brings another fantastic view of the waves crashing against the rocks. You might want to slip down to the beach and dip your toes in the water; be aware, however, that with waves and riptides the water along here can be very dangerous.

At Natural Bridges, lock your bike and take a walk out on the beach to look at the sandstone arch sculpted by time and wind and waves. Then head up the beach to look at the tidal pools where sea anemonae and starfish reside. A natural preserve, these tidal pools are among the best in the area and are only for looking, not collecting.

You can return to the Pier by cutting across town. Highway 1 becomes Mission Avenue, and it runs into Pacific Avenue. Follow Pacific through Pacific Garden Mall and stop off at Cooper House. The old Court House has been converted, the judges' chambers replaced with boutiques, specialty shops, restaurants and an outdoor garden restaurant where sidewalk entertainers — musicians, singers and poets — do their thing. Some really fine stained glass window treatment has been used in Cooper House.

Or from Natural Bridges just reverse yourself and pedal back along West Cliff Drive. This is one of those routes which looks totally different ridden in the opposite direction. The ride is especially great if it is late afternoon as the sun slips into the sea making silver sparkles on the water and brilliant orange streaks in the sky.

West Cliff Drive

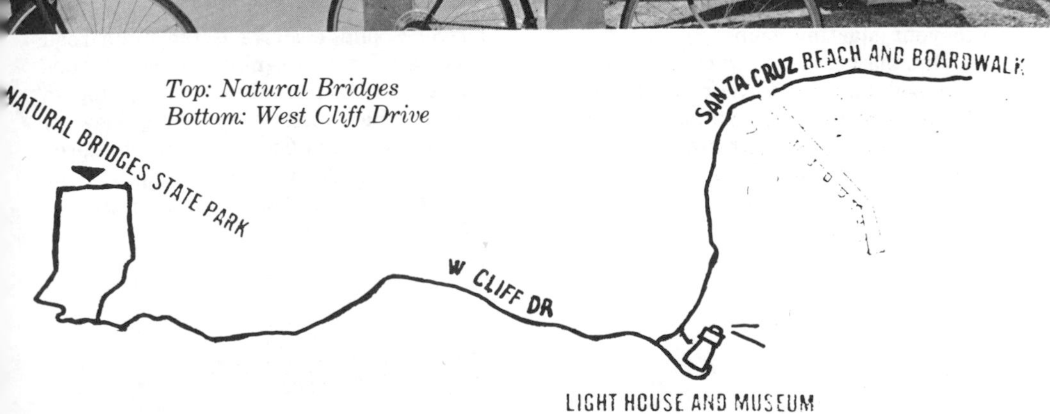

Top: Natural Bridges
Bottom: West Cliff Drive

SANTA CRUZ: On a Clear Day

On a clear day you can see forever, from the rolling meadowland of the University of California to Monterey Bay. If you are lucky enough to hit a clear sunny day in Santa Cruz this bike loop is especially enjoyable. The distance is either six or 12 miles, depending on the route you choose.

Start from the University of California at Santa Cruz main entrance parking lot. The buildings here on Bay Drive are part of the old Henry Cowell Ranch and have been preserved intact. Take Bay Drive—all downhill—to Mission Street, and then the Mission by-pass off Highway 1. This is part of Santa Cruz's famous Tree Sea Tour and the route is clearly marked to Natural Bridges State Beach.

Natural Bridges State Beach is one of the most beautiful spots on the Santa Cruz coast, with naturally eroded sandstone arches. Up the beach are many rocks that make particularly fine tidepools at low tide. If you watch for a while and learn how to look, you will find marine creatures in even the smallest pools. This is part of a marine preserve, for looking only, not collecting. Be sure to bike over to the far entrance and ask the ranger for directions to the Monarch Butterfly Trail. The monarchs migrate each year to a sheltered cove in red gum trees at the state beach.

Now, bike back to Western Drive which is an uphill trek to the UC campus. At the Western-High Street intersection you can turn right to return to your starting point.

But the best is yet to come, if you have the pedal power to tour the beautifully forested Santa Cruz campus. A scenic 1½ mile campus bike path starts at the main entrance on High Street, by-passes the Student Farm Project and the Lower Quarry, and terminates just below the Performing Arts complex in the central campus core. This pretty pathway climbs through meadowland, utilizing historic Red Hill Road which once served as the connecting link between Santa Cruz and Bonny Doon.

A trio of self-guiding walking tours, which are easily adapted to bike riding, is available free for the asking at the Campus Activities Office on the second floor of the Redwood Building above the Upper Quarry Parking Lot. Each tour points out the sculpture, the historic buildings, the buildings open to the public, and the art exhibits which visitors are invited to see. A yellow map that shows the developed part of the campus is available at the Visitor Information kiosk at the campus entrance.

The campus is designed in a way that makes bike riding the only way to go. The Santa Cruz plan of cluster colleges insures biking as the natural way to move from one part of the hilly campus to another. There are footpaths, bike lanes and little bridges that crisscross arroyos and cut through the clusters of redwood, oak and madrone trees. With elevation at the lowest point on campus at 285 feet, and the highest at 1,951, the terrain provides some challenging grades for 10-speed devotees as well as spectacular sites like those overlooking Monterey Bay.

In the central part of the campus, Heller Avenue loops around to McLaughlin Avenue, which cuts into Coolidge Drive. Coolidge Drive is the main road that takes you downhill to the campus entrance. About midway down, stop to admire the fantastic sweeping view of the city of Santa Cruz and the Monterey Bay beyond. The entire trip can be done in half a day and bike paths mark the entire route.

Top: Looking over Santa Cruz and Monterey Bay from UC Santa Cruz
Middle: Entrance UC campus
Bottom: Surrounded by ranch land

OLD SOQUEL: Mountaineering

If mountains are your thing—and you are a seasoned, experienced bike rider—then you are ready for the old Soquel-Santa Cruz Highway. Reserved for the best bicyclers only is the route from Soquel over Summit Road to Lexington Reservoir near Los Gatos.

The reward is beautiful mountain scenery, curvy little-traveled roads, and a ride that goes virtually up (to Summit Road) and then down (Old Santa Cruz Highway to Highway 17.)

Be careful and alert at all times. These are not wide roads and bikers should use extreme caution because motorists really aren't expecting to meet bicycles on these roads.

Start from the Soquel turnoff at Highway 1 in Capitola. This is Porter Street which becomes Old San Jose Road. The first few miles cover pretty rolling countryside with a gradual uphill swing. Stop off at the Soquel Forest Fire Station for your first rest and a visit. The firemen are on duty year around and welcome visitors.

Now the route begins to climb seriously upward, and there are great open spaces with fantastic views of the mountains beyond. Find a sunny open spot to stop and rest and enjoy the view. There are some pretty stands of redwood trees and open meadowland along here.

It is 14 miles uphill to Summit Road

and the first public facilities—a small shopping center where you can get a snack and a drink. Now you have two choices. If you want a loop route, you can turn around and be a "downhill rider" back to Capitola and your starting point. Or, you can continue to Lexington Reservoir on the Santa Clara Valley side of the mountain.

Follow Summit Road northwest for three miles to Old Santa Cruz Highway and turn right. This is strictly downhill all the way, with sharp blind turns, and it is amazing how many redwood trees line this very pretty shady road. The road takes great hairpin turns around some trees, for the men who built this route cared more to save the trees than to follow any straight roadway. The old highway curves and twists past now-abandoned Holy City and then scans the edge of Lexington Reservoir.

This is a good pickup spot if someone is meeting you because there is parking here. If you still have the energy, climb one last hill to Highway 17, where the new Santa Cruz Highway and the Old Santa Cruz Highway intersect. A sign says "STOP," because no bikers are allowed beyond this point.

This is a 23-mile one-way trip recommended for 10-speed (or more) bikes only. The faint-of-heart and novice riders would do well to pass it up.

Upper: Lexington Reservoir
Lower: Old Soquel Road

(19) BRANCIFORTE DRIVE: Downhill all the Way

One of the popular rides in the Santa Cruz Mountains is down Branciforte Drive through the dark green coolness of redwood stands, past the apple orchards, maples and sycamores. The route is downhill all the way, but at a reasonable rate of decline so that the trail is a leisurely pedal, at its best in spring when the wild flowers dot the hills and the blossoms break out, and in autumn when the madrones and toyons are heavy with red berries and the bushy-tailed tree squirrels are busy with their fall chores.

Start at Highway 17 where Vine Hill Road slides off to the left. Vine Hill becomes Branciforte. You could reverse the direction and climb the mountain from Market Street in Santa Cruz, but downhill is recommended for in this direction you pedal eight miles past small farms, old vineyards and the edge of DeLaveaga Park, a fine spot for a picnic.

Vine Hill Road is a narrow but maneuverable road two miles long which becomes Branciforte Drive at St. Clare's Retreat. Near the beginning of the ride you will see the old Vine Hill Schoolhouse, now a private residence with the 1883 date above the entrance. Redwood trees shade much of the route. As you drop down for the final descent past Happy Valley School, watch for the right turn indicating The Mystery Spot. The Mystery Spot is noted for numerous variations in gravity, perspective, velocity and height that are intriguing. Even the trees here do not appear to stand perpendicularly. The Spot is open daily from 9:30 A.M. to 5 A.M. and admission is $1.50.

Now pedal back out to Branciforte and continue down the hill. On the left along here is George Washington Memorial Grove, marking the edge of DeLaveaga Park. Playgrounds, restrooms, picnic spots and hiking trails are located in this mountain park. The park also contains one of Santa Cruz County's three historic covered bridges. In 1940 the Old Glen Canyon covered bridge was moved from its original site to the present location spanning Branciforte Creek. This bridge and the other two, at Felton and in Paradise Park, date back to the horse and buggy days and were constructed with the idea of protecting the bridge timbers from the heavy rains which fall in the Santa Cruz Mountains. Bikers and hikers are the only ones to use the bridge now and you can ride across it into DeLaveaga Park to reach the picnic area under the oaks and laurels.

Along the lowest portion of Branciforte you begin to see new homes popping up, and just under Highway 1 freeway the road becomes Market Street as you enter downtown Santa Cruz. You can stay on this road to work your way down to the Twin Lakes beach area.

If you prefer a loop route and don't mind some uphill climbs, start at De Laveaga Park, pedal to St. Clare's Retreat turnoff, and then bike back down to the park, a distance of ten miles.

Covered bridge

Upper: De Laveaga Creek
Lower: De Laveaga Park

(20)

FELTON: Henry Cowell Park

Roaring Camp Railroad

There are bike paths just begging to be ridden, and the trail through Henry Cowell Redwood State Park in Felton is one of them. The forest of Henry Cowell Park looks much the same today as it did 200 years ago when Zayante Indians found shelter and game here. The Indians left the mountains for Santa Cruz Mission life, but the beauty and solitude of the forest they once knew is still here to be enjoyed, especially by bicycle.

The first bike path to cut directly through the park is now open. Called Pipe Line Road, it is the only path designated for bike use. It is three miles plus 15 feet long and cuts from Park Headquarters to the edge of the park at Graham Hill Road.

Pedaling the ups and downs of Pipe Line Trail can be strenuous—you go up, then coast down. There is one particularly steep spot. But is worth every labored breath, for this is a fascinating closeup view of towering coast redwood trees and park plant life, shrouded in a foggy mantle of coolness. You will meet few other riders.

At the edge of the park you can turn around and pedal your way back, for you get a whole different perspective of the 1,737-acre park going in the reverse direction.

Or, you can ride Graham Hill Road north to loop around the park back to Highway 9, returning to the main entrance of the park again. This is a distance of ten miles. Graham Hill Road is a busy, often dangerous thoroughfare, and riders with children along would do well to avoid the route and ride back on Pipe Line Trail.

The Henry Cowell ride has an extra bonus. The Roaring Camp and Big Trees Narrow-Gauge Railroad is adjacent to the park and is especially popular with railroad buffs of any age. The steam train departs each hour, puffing its way through the redwood forest. The locomotive pulls the open excursion cars up the steepest railroad grades in the West, from Roaring Camp to Bear Mountain, through points colorfully called such names as Big Trees, Indian Creek, Grizzly Flats and Deer Valley, where you can sometimes see deer grazing. At Bear Mountain you can stop over to picnic and hike before returning on a later train.

Round trip railroad fare is $3.50 for adults; half fare for children 3 to 15; free under 3. There is a $1 day use fee at Henry Cowell Park. The main entrance to park headquarters, the redwood grove, picnic area and Pipe Line Trail all are located off Highway 9 in Felton, near Santa Cruz.

If a weekend campout is on your schedule, there is a campground at the park. Advance reservations are needed for overnight camping at the 51-unit Graham Hill campground. There are a number of other good bike trails to explore on a weekend visit to Felton.

HENRY COWELL
REDWOODS
STATE PARK

REDWOOD
GROVE

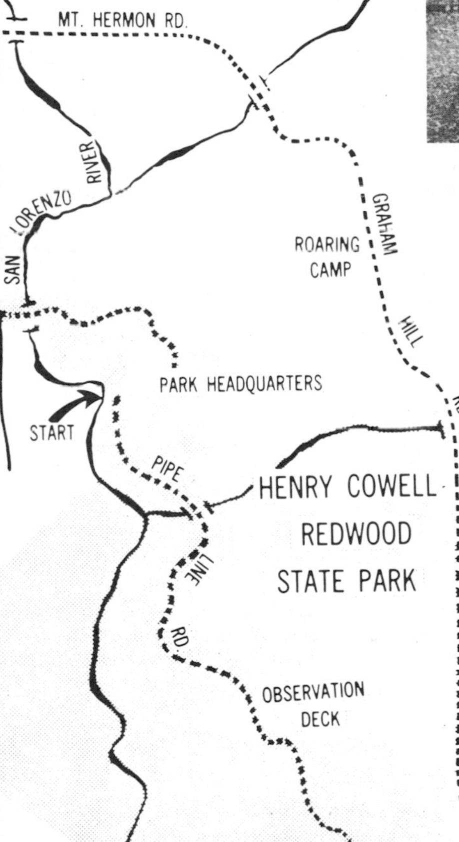
MT. HERMON RD.
SAN LORENZO RIVER
GRAHAM HILL RD.
ROARING CAMP
PARK HEADQUARTERS
START
PIPE LINE RD.
HENRY COWELL
REDWOOD
STATE PARK
OBSERVATION
DECK

FELTON: Trail Goes On and On

Some bike trails seem to go on forever. Highway 9 through the Santa Cruz Mountains is one of those. You can pedal around to your heart's content, back-tracking, looping, crisscrossing and exploring some of the prettiest redwood country along the San Lorenzo River.

The Covered Bridge in Felton is an old historic spot and makes a natural starting point. You can park near here without cost, unload your bike and ride on Graham Hill Road to Highway 9.

Head northwest along the winding roadway that follows the river. On weekends this is a busy route but bikers abound anyway. Sometimes the road widens, as when it passes through the towns, but much of Highway 9 has only a narrow shoulder to bike on, and you must heed the cars and trucks that hurry by.

On this "go on forever" route you can go on to Ben Lomond (three miles) or on to Boulder Creek (six miles) or on to Big Basin (16 miles). Or, if you are a mountain climber, you can continue to Saratoga Gap and back to San Jose on a route that goes very nearly straight up from Boulder Creek to the Gap, and then straight down into Saratoga and San Jose.

Wherever your handlebars lead you, all of this area is tremendously pretty redwood country with hilly ups and downs and numerous bridges spanning the river.

In the town of Ben Lomond there are lots of little shops to explore. Turn into town on Mill Street and visit the Park (Ben Lomond Recreation District), where the San Lorenzo River is dammed for swimming and there are a sandy beach and lawn for sunning yourself.

Boulder Creek is a pleasant vacation town and in the summer visitors make it headquarters for warm summer days. San Lorenzo River goes through the center of town and as you ride along Highway 9 you are threading along the edge of the river.

Outside of Boulder Creek, the roadway begins some serious uphill climbing. You can stay on Highway 9 to head uphill to Saratoga Gap at the Summit Road, or you can veer to the left following the trail to Big Basin. The ride crests a ridge and then drops down to the basin at Park Headquarters. This state park is famous for its beautiful redwood groves.

There are numerous side roads off Highway 9 and you can be adventuresome and go exploring on your own. Most roads loop around and back down to Highway 9 at some point, and there are miles and miles of deserted, picturesque mountain roads to explore.

Near Felton, these dogs are friendly

Swimming beach, Ben Lomond

Felton by Big Basin

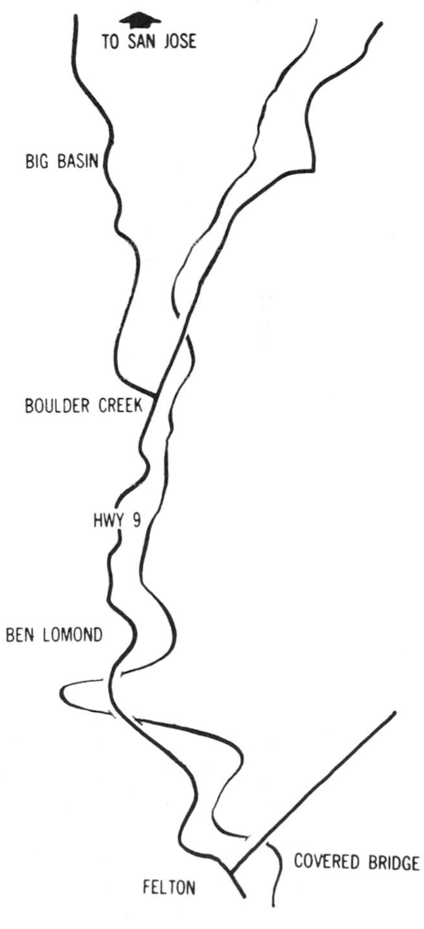

BIG BASIN: They Saved the Redwoods

When Big Basin was made the first of the California State Parks, the dream was to "save the redwoods from the Skyline to the ocean." Today the dream is a reality. Big Basin State Park on the ocean-facing slopes of the Santa Cruz Mountains covers about 12,000 acres, mostly within the Waddell Creek Watershed. A backpacking and horse trail from the Castle Rock portion of the park at the Skyline weaves its way down the slope through Big Basin to the Pacific Ocean.

You can see much of the beauty of Big Basin from the seat of a bicycle, for the easy-sloped paved roadways within the park are open to bike riders. Experienced riders might want to ride to Big Basin from another location, but both the approach from Saratoga Gap at the Skyline and Highway 9 from Santa Cruz are tough mountain rides. The easiest thing to do is drive to Big Basin, unload your bike at the Ranger Station, and make this the starting point for a one- or two-day bike ride.

The heart of the park is located in the Opal Creek flatlands at the very bottom of Big Basin. The park headquarters are located here, along with a little museum known as the Nature Lodge. There is also a store and gift shop which is open during summer months. The Nature Lodge houses a fine collection of historical and natural science exhibits, and Columbian black-tailed deer can usually be seen wandering in the meadow.

The lure of Big Basin, of course, is in the magnificent redwood stands saved from the sawmills by the Sempervirens Club at the turn of the century. One of the park's most ancient and impressive redwood groves is located at Opal Creek and a self-guiding nature trail points out some of its most notable features. There is an extensive interpretative program carried on at this park, and the rangers are more than happy to point sightseers in the right direction. There are 35 miles of hiking trails; bikers may ride only on the paved roadways, but these provide a more than adequate view of the basin. But if the lure of Sempervirens Falls, McAbee Mountain Overlook, or the Middleridge, which was used by the Costanoan Indians hunting grizzly, becomes too appealing, you will have to lock your bike and explore these by foot.

At Park Headquarters ask for the Basin Brochure which shows the numerous trails. Using this as your guide, you can explore by bike along the roadway lining the Sequoia Trail—it follows Waddell Creek—to Sky Meadow and Slippery Rock. This road loops around to pick up Lodge Road, which at one time was the original way into Big Basin. You can either ride as far as Lodge Road to see the beauty spots of the park and then reverse yourself and ride back, or you can pedal a hilly distance around onto Highway 236 to return to the park.

Another bike route picks up the Skyline-to-the-Sea Trail—you are biking up, but the backpackers are hiking down the final slope of the 23-mile climb from Castle Rock to the park. The ride threads Opal Creek along Trail Beautiful. As you ride along here, you can see black scars and burned areas on the redwoods. They are from the fires of 1851 and 1904, which burned almost all of Big Basin except the area immediately around the headquarters. Trail Beautiful is one of the park's oldest trails and its name gives promise of what is to be seen. As this road works upward past Rogers Creek it cuts over to pick up Highway 236, the main entryway into the park. The main roadway is a grand downhill sweep into the basin redwoods.

At the Ranger Station you can also obtain "Short Historic Tours," which describes automobile tours adaptable to experienced bike riders, as well as some shorter tours.

con't

Deer may welcome you

Big Basin, where virgin timber stands

You can bike at Big Basin all year ng. Summer riding is best although oth spring and autumn bring their own eculiar beauty to the redwood forest. In inter some of the outer paved roads ay be closed so you are limited where ou might pedal, although you can go nywhere you choose on foot.

There are 200 campsites so a bike-ampout is a logical choice. Restrooms nd hot showers are available. Campsite eservations are needed (from 10 to 90 ays in advance) and the 158 picnic sites re available on a first-come-first-served asis.

COAST RIDE: Fifty Miles of Beach

Along the 50 miles from Santa Cruz north to Half Moon Bay is some outstanding beach biking. Along here Highway 1 borders some of the best surf and beaches in the region, gloriously deserted during the week, but a haven for beach devotees on the weekend. The beautiful part is that you don't have to bike the whole 50 miles to reap the rewards. You can begin and end anywhere it suits you, starting with an easy ten-mile pedal along mostly flat land and expanding the ride to whatever distance matches your endurance.

The easiest bike riding segment is the stretch of Highway 1 between Pigeon Point Lighthouse and Pescadero Beach. This is a wide handsome highway with a good shoulder for biking. At Pigeon Point the Coast Guard Lighthouse welcomes visitors. This section of rocky beach is well-known to rock hunters, and petrified whale bone is one of the good finds easily spotted.

North of Pigeon Point, the flat road edges the beach but some of the beachside property is fenced as private residences. Bean Hollow State Beach has restrooms and some interesting rock finds. The rocks on the beach are as tiny as beans and each one is a shiny treasure weathered from a rock formation offshore. Both Bean Hollow and Pebble Beach have the same rocks and from either one you can take home a pocketful of rocks, put them in a jar of water and enjoy watching how the water brings out the colors.

The road hardly veers from the rocky coast that takes you to Pescadero Beach. Pescadero means "the fishing place" and the beach is popular with fishermen who cast their lines into the surf from the rock formations extending into the sea.

For a longer route of about 20 miles, start from Waddell Creek and pedal north to Pescadero. Waddell Creek has formed a long gentle sandy beach and surfers ride the waves here. You will pedal uphill toward Elephant Rock and then drop down to Ano Nuevo State Beach. Be sure to use the public road and not the private ranch road to pedal out to the beach for a good view of the island where seals, sea lions and an occasional walrus reside.

The road curves inland as it crosses into San Mateo County and then reaches back to brush the shore of Gazos Beach at Butano State Park. From here, it begins its easy sweeping curve to Pigeon Point Lighthouse.

Consider going the whole distance if you are ready to join the 50-mile-a-day riders. Start from Natural Bridges State Beach in Santa Cruz. Highway 1 remains remarkably flat until it makes its up-and-down approach to Davenport. Bikers in January have a good chance to see the migrating grey whales as they pass by the beach at Davenport and whale-watching is a serious endeavor here. Some whales are close enough to be studied through binoculars. From Davenport the road is rather hilly until it reaches Waddell Creek.

From Pescadero Beach, Highway 1 becomes much more hilly with climbs and dips between the Pomponio and San Gregorio State Beaches. After San Gregorio, Highway 1 works back from the beach through fields of Brussels sprouts and artichokes. As you enter the town of Half Moon Bay, follow the fork on the right off Highway 1 to pedal downtown. Along Main Street are some good eating places and interesting shops.

HALF MOON BAY
TUNITAS
SAN GREGORIO BEACH
PESCADERO
PESCADERO PT.
PEBBLE BEACH
PIGEON PT.
LIGHT STATION
ANO NUEVO PT.
DAVENPORT
SANTA CRUZ
NATURAL BRIDGES

ANO NUEVO BEACH
STATE PARK
WARNING TO PUBLIC
DUE TO EXTREMELY DANGEROUS
TIDAL CURRENTS AND HIDDEN
REEFS, ALL PERSONS ARE
CROSSING TO ISLAND

Ano Nuevo Beach State Park, top, and Ano Nuevo Island—Note warning
Below: Beaches, Davenport

(24) KENNEDY ROAD: Pretty but Strenuous

One of the prettiest—and most strenuous—bike loops in Los Gatos is the trip over Kennedy and Shannon Roads. Over the six-mile route, the rider will encounter narrow roads, steep inclines and switchbacks. The scenery and the thrill of the downhill sweeps more than make up for the taxing climbs.

The corner of Englewood and Shannon Roads makes a good starting point for the loop, moving along the attractive residential area to the arterial stop at Kennedy Road. Make a left turn and start the uphill climb at a gradual pace. You might have to get off and walk a bit, alternating pedaling and walking. Good use of uphill gears will ease the strain. Stay in the center at the intersection of South Kennedy Road, Kennedy, and Longmeadow Drive.

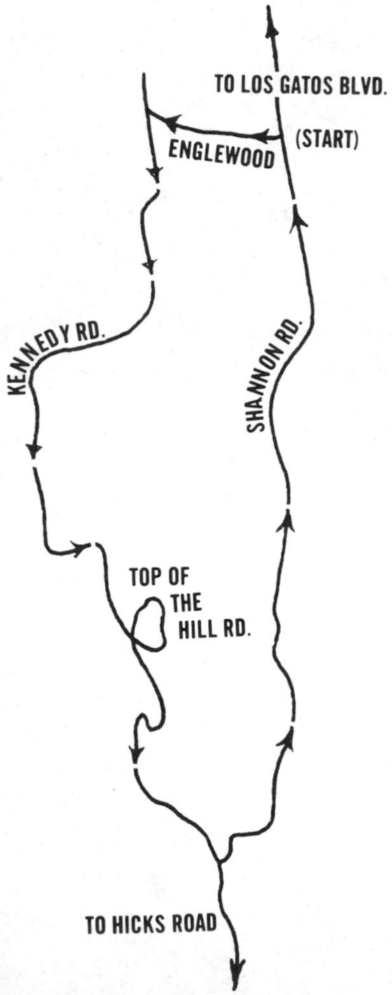

Just above this intersection is a sunny meadow, the property of a boarding stable, with the horses chasing each other. This is a good spot to take a breather before starting the tree-shaded climb to the top of the ridge where a beautiful view of the hills and valleys stretches out in every direction.

Steep switchbacks take the rider down the ridge to the intersection of Shannon Road. Good brakes are a must. At the intersection, turn left again, and move back over the ridge. The climb here is steep but relatively short. The downhill slope is winding but with less pitch than Kennedy.

The best time to ride this route is during the morning hours when there is less traffic, since both roadways are narrow and drivers aren't expecting bike riders on the curves. This is an especially pretty ride in the springtime when wild flowers dot the meadows, and in the autumn when the bold strokes of orange and yellow color the land. There are no rest stops as such on the route, but there are many wide spots in the road where you can pull off and admire the view. If you want refreshments you will have to tote them along, so take a canteen and lunch.

Kennedy Road at Longmeadow Drive

Farm and wooded areas abound

(25)

LOS GATOS: Vasona

Vasona Lake in Los Gatos is the most natural starting point for any bike tour of the Los Gatos region. Located right off Highway 17, Vasona Lake has all things good: pretty surroundings, boating, fishing, restrooms, picnic facilities and playground. In the afternoon when the wind sweeps toward the foothills, kites dance in the sky, for Vasona has the reputation for being one of the best kite-flying areas around.

From Vasona, bike along the creek through Oak Meadow Park, where the Billy Jones Steam Railroad is a special attraction in summer. Then follow University Avenue for two miles to Old Town in downtown Los Gatos. On a busy weekend at Old Town you can watch artists at work in this Spanish-style converted grammar school that now houses 40 unique shops and boutiques, plus restaurants and a performing arts theater.

Pedal around downtown Los Gatos. For art lovers, three art galleries offer the best of the local artists: Los Gatos Art Association and Gallery, 21 University Avenue, open Tuesday through Sunday, free; El Gatito Art Gallery, 123 West Main Street, open Tuesday through Friday, free; Group 21, 100 West Main Street, open daily, free.

If old things appeal to you, visit the Los Gatos Museum, Main Street and Tait Avenue. It is open daily without cost.

Now follow Tait Avenue downhill to Highway 9, turn left, and bike 4½ miles to Villa Montalvo. There are some portions along busy Highway 9 which have paths off the highway for bikes.

Villa Montalvo always has special exhibits on view in the art gallery. The Villa is the former home of the late Senator James Phelan and now houses traveling art and craft exhibits, work by resident artists, and interesting displays. The Villa is open daily until 5 P.M. and docents are available for guided tours of the grand house.

Sailboats on Vasona Lake

The grounds of Montalvo are maintained as an arboretum and the landscaped grounds coupled with beautiful Greek statuary make this a great bike route. You can pedal around the paved roadways at Montalvo but must park your bike to hike the landscaped paths.

From Montalvo turn right onto Highway 9 to return to Vasona Lake by way of University Avenue. This is about 14 miles round trip.

Old Town at Los Gatos.

Villa Montalvo in Saratoga

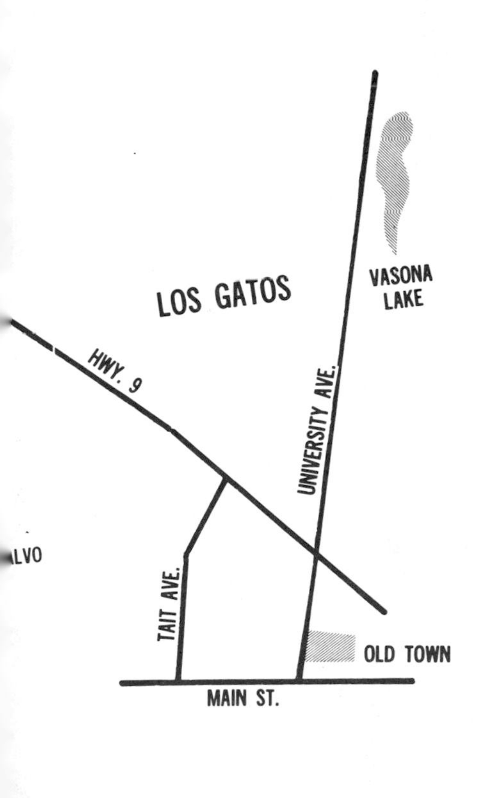

SARATOGA: The Wine Tour

Whatever bike route winds through Saratoga, Villa Montalvo must be included. It only makes sense, then, to start and finish a bike route from the beautiful Villa. Take Highway 9 off Highway 17 in Los Gatos and watch for the great stone pillars which mark the Montalvo site.

Start this ten-mile loop from the parking lot of Villa Montalvo. No bikes are allowed on the Montalvo trails, but you can ride through the main grounds, view the natural arboretum maintained on the grounds by Santa Clara County Parks Department, look at the art exhibits and displays housed in the Villa, and admire the Greek statues and other stone work around the Villa grounds.

Ride out the Villa grounds exit (it is one way only) and turn right onto Saratoga-Los Gatos Road. Follow this route to Fruitvale Avenue where a left turn onto Fruitvale leads to some off-highway paths. Turn right onto Allendale for a leisurely ride across West Valley College campus, where great old oak trees provide shade.

Follow Allendale to Quito Road and turn left. Stay on the off-highway paths past Quito School and watch for Cox Avenue, which is a left turn only. Take Cox to Saratoga Avenue.

The Paul Masson Winery on Saratoga Avenue makes a good stopover, especially if Dad came along for the ride. Hourly tours are from 10 A.M. to 4 P.M. daily, and the wine-tasting room is open the same hours. The conducted tour includes an interesting explanation of how the famous Paul Masson champagne is made in the Champagne Cellars here.

Now follow Saratoga Avenue back to the city of Saratoga to the main intersection. Be sure to visit the old firehouse which is on this corner. There are numerous interesting shops and boutiques in the area, especially on Big Basin Way. You can buy a butter paddle, a tooled belt, or an original painting in the shops that line the wide walkways. Pedal back to Villa Montalvo on Highway 9. The last half mile will be the hardest because it is uphill to the Villa.

If you still have the energy after the ten-mile ride, a walk through some of the beautiful Montalvo woods is a fitting climax.

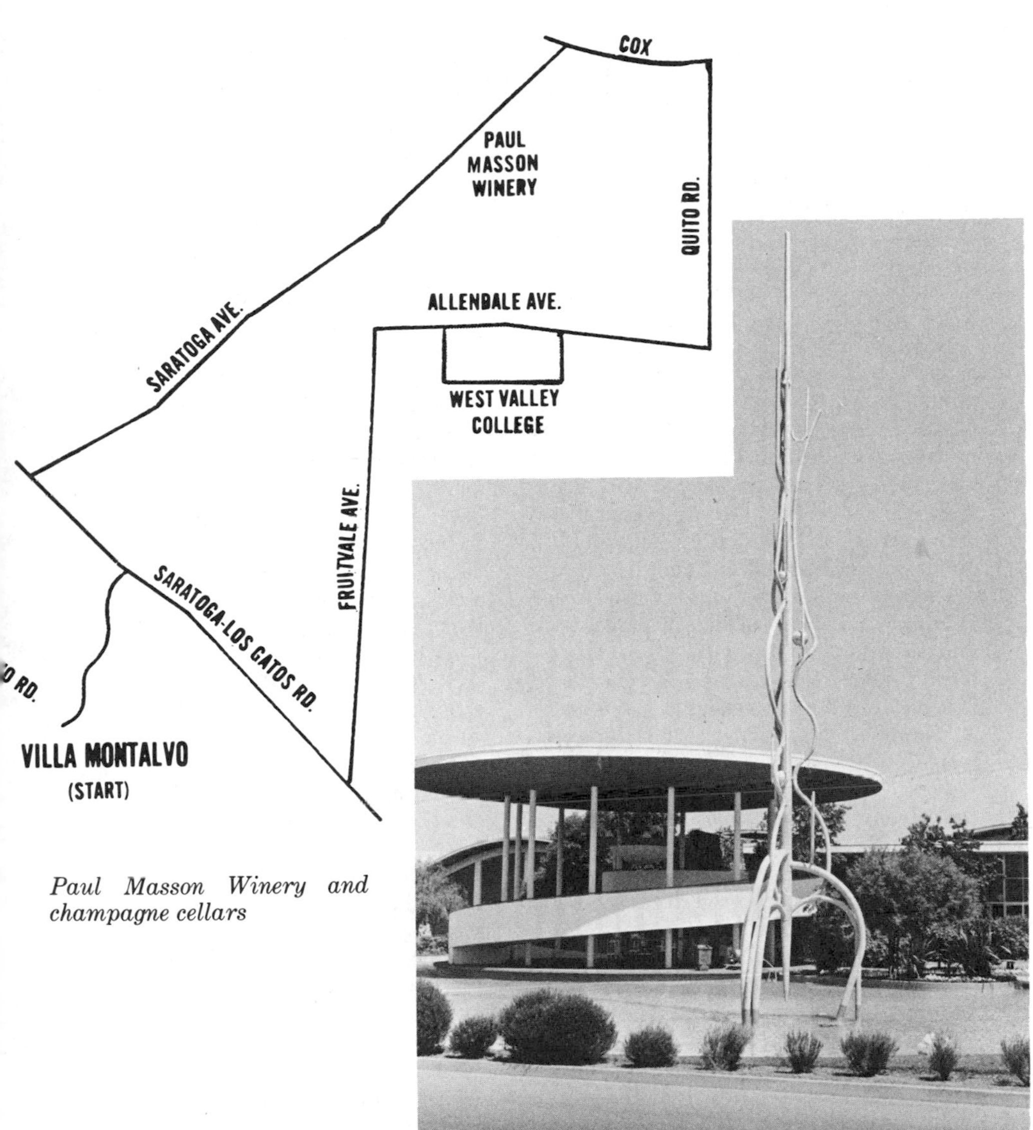

Paul Masson Winery and champagne cellars

Going there

Los Gatos Junction

SARATOGA: Gardener's Delight

The "gardener's delight bike ride" in Saratoga covers three of the most beautiful parks in the Santa Clara Valley. Within a 12-mile pedaling distance of each other (round trip) are Hakone Gardens, Saratoga Community Garden and Villa Montalvo.

Hakone Gardens, 21000 Big Basin Way, Saratoga, makes a good starting point. Parking space for cars is somewhat limited at Hakone, but you may park in the Village Public Parking Lot located on Fourth Street off Big Basin Way. The hill back up Big Basin will serve as a good warm-up for the hill going up to Hakone Gardens.

Hakone is a Japanese hill-and-water garden located on an old 17-acre estate and now part of the City of Saratoga's public parks. The garden is considered remarkable for its rare natural beauty achieved in unity with the Japanese house on the slope of the Moon-Viewing Hill. In form, Hakone is landscaped in the strolling pond style typical of the Japanese gardens of the middle 17th century.

For those walking through Hakone, the naturalness is a rare treat. Hakone is not the typical American park in that no eating is allowed except in the tea room, which is open to the public. Tea and soft drinks plus Oriental cookies and crackers are available.

The ride down the hill from Hakone to Big Basin Way is very steep so be sure your brakes are in good working order. Then pedal down to Highway 9, turn right and continue two miles on Highway 9 to Villa Montalvo, which is clearly marked.

Montalvo is probably one of the best-known sites in the area. The grounds of Montalvo are maintained as an arboretum by Santa Clara County Parks and Recreation Department and have been planted with many rare trees and shrubs.

The roads and trails of Montalvo interlace the arboretum, giving access to the extensive plantings and natural flora. Most recently developed is the Nature Trail, a self-guiding path more than a mile in length.

You may ride your bike only on the paved roadways. You must explore by foot the other trails, and it is interesting to note the transition zones from dry chaparral to larger woodland, the flora becoming larger the nearer it is to the shady moist redwood area.

A Nature Trail guide, keyed to explain what you see along the trail, is available from the park office. In addition, Greek statues, plus a gazebo and a Greek temple, add to the formal mood of the Montalvo grounds. The Villa is open daily to visitors; there is usually a number of art and craft displays on view. There is no picnicking at Montalvo.

Now ride out Montalvo Road (a one-way road) to Highway 9. Turn right onto Highway 9 and then left onto Fruitvale Avenue. The Community Garden, sponsored by the City of Saratoga, is located on ten acres of property leased from the International Order of Odd Fellows (IOOF). Entrance to the garden is located off Fruitvale Avenue near San Marcos Road. It is a private road identified by the large horseshoe-shaped white iron gateway with the initials IOOF over the entrance.

con't

Hakone Gardens

The garden is mainly a demonstration garden used to teach people the proper methods of biodynamic gardening, and is open to the public from 9 A.M. to 5 P.M. Monday through Sunday. People may visit, take classes, or participate by working in the garden. Those who participate in work may share in the harvest.

Now continue on Fruitvale to Saratoga Avenue. Turn left onto Saratoga for a picturesque return to your starting point near Hakone Gardens.

At the end of the journey at Hakone, Wildwood Park is just across the street on the other side of the creek and is a good place for a picnic lunch. Restrooms are available at both Hakone and Wildwood.

Be sure to take your camera. The gardens are in pretty bloom all year around and you will want to record the scenes in color.

SANTA CLARA: Never on Monday

"Never on Monday" could be the rule for this easy bike ride, for on Monday some of the best attractions are closed to visitors. On any other day, you can pedal a pleasant eight miles through some of Santa Clara's oldest areas—a route that covers the Central Park complex, University of Santa Clara and Triton Museum.

Start at Central Park on Keily Boulevard. Here there is something for everyone: picnicking, a playground, a small lake with a fountain, tennis courts and nice open spaces. Here also Santa Clara International Swim Center, the home of champions, is open to the public during the summer when swim meets are not underway. The three-pool complex includes a diving well with underwater observation, and the Hall of Fame honors Olympic medal-winning area swimmers.

Bike across the park, through the swim center parking lot, turn left onto White Avenue and then right onto Benton Street. Tree-lined Benton is a direct route to downtown Santa Clara. Turn right onto Lafayette Street and left onto Franklin Street to reach the University of Santa Clara.

The University is built around the Mission in a lovely garden setting. You can visit DeSaisset Art Gallery and Museum, open without cost Tuesday through Friday from 10 A.M. to 5 P.M. and Saturday and Sunday from 1 to 4 P.M. It is closed Monday. DeSaisset houses an unusual collection of early California and Mission artifacts dating back to 1777; exhibits are of both modern and classical art.

Mission Santa Clara DeAsis is the central building on campus and is open to visitors daily. Founded in 1777, it is the eighth of California's 21 missions. Also, park your bike and walk through the campus rose gardens, which are especially beautiful and peaceful in late spring.

Now, pedal back to Lafayette and then turn right onto Washington Street. This wide old street is ideal for bike riding and there are some lovely old Victorian houses along the way. Turn left onto Civic Center Drive, and ride past the reflecting pool at Civic Center where Benny Bufano's statue of St. Clare centers the pool. Then turn right onto Lincoln Street to the Triton Museum of Art.

Triton sprawls over seven acres of landscaped gardens with four octagonal buildings holding most of the art work. The pavillion buildings are joined by landscaped walkways and courts decorated with sculpture. The museum is open to the public without cost Tuesday through Friday, 2:30 to 4:30 P.M., Saturday, 10 A.M. to 4 P.M. and Sunday from 1 to 4 P.M. It is closed Monday. Works in the permanent collection are displayed on a rotating basis. In addition, local artists display, usually for a month.

Behind the museum is the historic Jamison-Brown House. This Victorian house has been restored and is open to the public. The original inlaid woodwork on the second floor is a wonder of craftsmanship.

As you come out of the museum, go right on Warburton Avenue to Los Padres Boulevard. Turn left onto Los Padres and use the bike lane to travel back to Benton Street and then to Central Park.

Plan your ride to start early in the day so that you can cap it off with a swim at the International Swim Center. It is open daily during the summer from noon to 6 P.M.

Central Park, Santa Clara

Santa Clara Mission (left) and DeSaisset Gallery (right) on Santa Clara University campus

Statue at Triton Museum which is housed in octagonal building in background

TWO FAMOUS SITES: San Jose

Two of Santa Clara Valley's most famous sites are within an easily-pedaled four miles of each other, round trip—the Rosicrucian Egyptian Museum and the Winchester Mystery House. If you start early you can easily take in both sights with plenty of time to enjoy both. Start with the Rosicrucian Museum; plan to spend a couple of hours here.

Located at 1342 Naglee Avenue, at the corner of Park Avenue, the Rosicrucian Museum is open every day, from noon to 5 P.M. on Saturday, Sunday and Monday, and from 9 A.M. to 5 P.M. Tuesday through Friday. There is no charge. Rare and original Egyptian, Assyrian and Babylonian antiques are on display, and you can tour a replica of a 4,000-year-old Egyptian tomb. The art gallery, planetarium and science museum also are open daily. No bicycling is permitted on the inside grounds, but this is a lovely walk with paths weaving among fountains and flowers. Now ride on to the Municipal Rose Gardens, Naglee Avenue at Dana.

The Rose Gardens are open from 10 A.M. to 6:30 P.M. and offer the perfect spot for a picnic. Ride among the more than 150 varieties of fragrant and colorful roses in a natural setting of grassy knolls and tree-lined paths. The roses begin blooming in April and are at their best from then until early autumn.

Rosicrucian Museum

Continue on Naglee, which becomes Forest Avenue in the area of Valley Fair Shopping Center. Turn left onto Winchester Boulevard to go to the Winchester Mystery House.

Sarah Winchester's famous house is being completely restored and the sounds of the workmen's hammers may be heard, just as when Mrs. Winchester continually added rooms to the strange house, thinking the sounds of hammering would keep away evil spirits. Now only curious visitors wander through the house, and guided tours are given daily from 9 A.M., rain or shine.

If you haven't been here for a while, it is certainly worth a new visit. Most of the inside and outside of the house has been repainted, period furniture has been added to four rooms, the Winchester Rifle and Wax Museum is complete, and the gift shop, refreshments area and Mrs. Winchester's summer gazebo are all open.

There is a 1¼-hour tour of just the house, and a combination house and garden tour that takes 2½ hours. Admission is adults, $3; children 5 to 12, $1.50; and children under 5, free. Large bike groups—Scouts or whatever—get a group rate for more than 20 people.

For the return trip, take Winchester Boulevard through Santa Clara to Newhall Street. Watch for one of the right-turn side streets such as Sunny Vista, Boxwood or Tulip, and take this off Winchester for a nice ride through some pretty tree-lined residential streets. Any one of these streets cuts back into Newhall. Turn off Newhall Street onto Park Avenue for a direct route to Rosicrucian Museum.

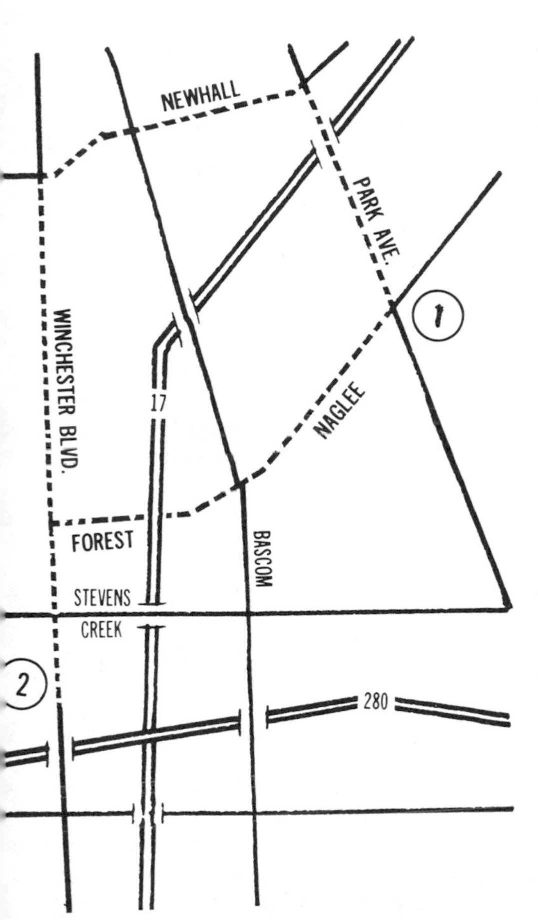

Winchester Mystery House

Young bike riders outside Rosicrucian Egyptian museum

COYOTE CREEK: For Bikers Only

Nestled alongside—and at one point under—the heavily trafficked Bayshore Freeway in South San Jose lies one of the prettiest and most secluded bike routes. The bike trail from Hellyer Park lines Coyote Creek along the Coyote Park Chain of the Santa Clara County Parks and Recreation development.

Paved and banked for bike traffic, the route winds along the east bank of Coyote Creek for six miles, through the park and then past farm land and orchards which still bank the creek. The only hazards are nature's—a branch on the trail or a squirrel darting across the path.

The bike trail starts near the Vellodrome located in the park. Drive past the Ranger Station and park in the first parking section on your left. The start of the bike trail is literally right in front of you. First segment of the trail follows the creek through the main part of the park. Hellyer Pond is the focal point here and fishermen are a common sight, trying for a bite. There are picnic tables, a play area and restrooms. Once the trail crosses under the freeway there are no more facilities of any kind to be found.

The six-foot-wide paved trail is uphill, but so gradual that you are hardly aware of it. On the right are old oak trees shading the creek. On the left is the tended farm land. Depending on the time of year, you will find farmers plowing, planting, irrigating or picking and packing the vegetables. You ride right past the packing house and this is a good spot to stop to rest while you watch the workers crating the harvest.

A horse trail follows a similar course to the bike trail. Along the way you will meet an occsional jogger and a few other bikers. For the most part the trail is all yours. The second section of the trail between Piercy and Tennant Roads passes the percolation ponds where Coyote Creek water has been rerouted into gravel ponds to seep down, helping to raise the water table of the valley. The fruit orchards are along here and the trail cuts right through them—an especially pretty spot in the springtime when the pink or white blossoms are on the fruit trees and the yellow mustard is growing wild. Along the third section, beyond Tennant Road, watch for the fishermen along the creek bank. Birds and ducks dart among the rushes in the water, and all you can see are the open spaces and the nearby mountains.

The trail ends at Coyote Dam, and during the hot days of summer this is like an oasis at the end of the trail. Water tumbles over the spillway and splashes around the big rocks. You can walk down some steps to the water's edge and cool your feet, or just sit on the bank and take in the restful sight. Soon another three-mile section of the trail will be completed, taking the biker along the edge of the lake to additional percolation ponds further up the creek.

The ride is best as an out-and-back trip along the trail, and even young bikers can manage this pleasant 12 miles. A rider could, however, leave the trail at Tennant Road, taking the narrow roadways following Piercy Road, Coyote Road and Palisade Drive back to Hellyer Park entrance.

The Vellodrome, while you are in the park, is worth investigating. If you are lucky, bike riders will be practicing on the Vellodrome and you can watch the skilled riders whipping past at a frightening speed. Designed primarily for competitive riding, it is a large, paved, banked oval. It is available for use on a schedule basis, with proper release and equipment. More information can be obtained from the park rangers at Hellyer.

Coyote Creek Bike Trail

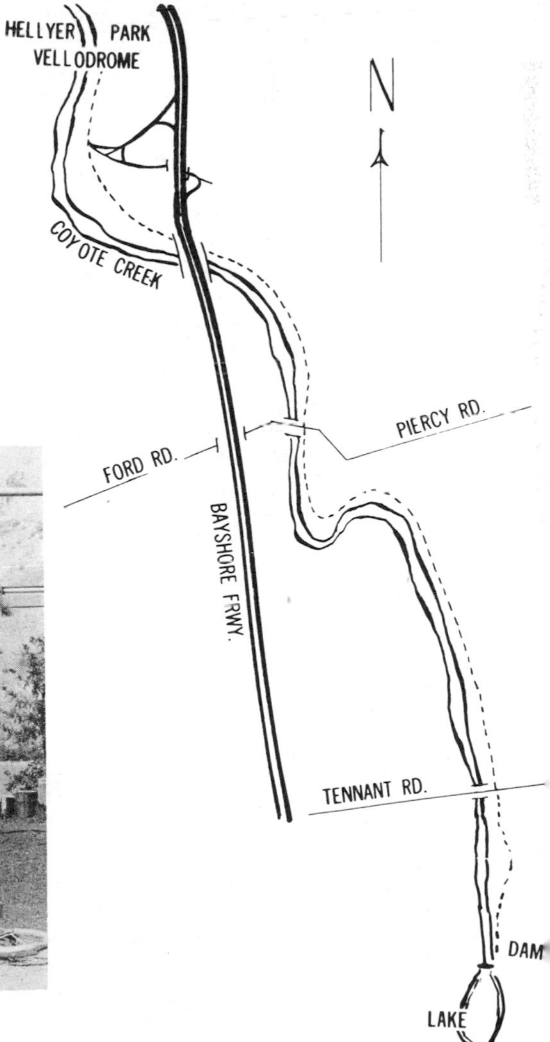

Coyote Creek Park

(31) EVERGREEN VALLEY: Country Riding

As you pedal along the winding country roads of Evergreen Valley, you have the feeling that you have turned back the calendar to the time that orchardists and farmers dominated Santa Clara Valley. Evergreen is the last rural stronghold in San Jose, with cows and picturesque old barns on hills the color of polished jade, which reveal how Evergreen got its name. For most of the season, the foothills southeast of San Jose are covered with grass—irrigated, of course, in the hot months of summer, but nonetheless green.

Take Capitol Expressway off Highway 101 and then San Felipe Road to Evergreen Valley College for your starting point. From the campus, bike along the creek road and then turn left onto San Felipe Road. After you pass the Villages, San Felipe becomes a rural road, following the contour of the hills through a canyon and beyond to sheep and cattle grazing country. After San Felipe passes Silver Creek Road, the route begins to climb, bisecting eucalyptus groves at some points. The final one-half mile to the summit is the steepest portion, and from here it drops in a steady banked descent past Metcalf Road turnoff. The highlight of this segment is riding under some magnificent old eucalyptus trees which almost form a tunnel over parts of the road.

After you reach the ranch, turn around and ride back on San Felipe Road over the summit. Near the bottom of the hill on the return ride, watch for Silver Creek Road, the only left turn you can make. Silver Creek follows the south side of the hill at a gradual downhill rate. The same type of rolling hills, arroyos and clumps of oak add to the pleasant country setting. As you come down the last foothill to the flatland you have a great view of the entire Santa Clara Valley, as far as Moffett Field on a clear day. On a smoggy day, you are lucky to see the bottom of the hill.

As you pedal through the residential section past Silver Creek High School, turn right onto King Road to cross Capitol Expressway (no biking on the Expressway) and pick up Aborn Road, watching for the beginning of San Felipe Road. This will take you through the community of Evergreen and past its few stores.

If you use the San Felipe-Silver Creek Road loop, you will pedal ten miles. If you try the hill-climbing portion to work your way to the ranch and back again, you will have biked 21 miles. Spring is the best time to ride this route. The valley is very hot during the summer months when the temperature in the canyons soars.

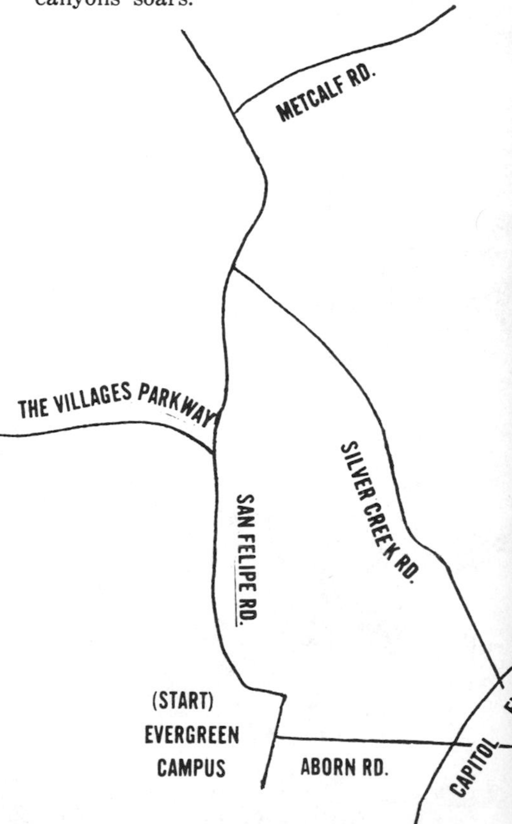

icturesque rural scenery

SAN JOSE: Kelley Park

From Kelley Park you can ride to downtown San Jose to view some of the city's best sights. Kelley Park at Keyes and Senter Road is the ideal starting point, but you may become so enamored with the Kelley Park complex that you get no further than these 150 acres of gentle rolling hills and tree-lined picnic spots.

Kelley Park is the home of the San Jose Baby Zoo where the animals are as near as the few inches it takes to stretch your hand to pet them. Stanley, the smiling llama, is one of the best-known residents of the zoo. Too, Happy Hollow Children's Park is open daily with rides, attractions, and the Happy Hollow Puppeteers. There is a small fee for admission.

From Happy Hollow you can bike across the park to the Japanese Friendship Garden on Senter Road, open Tuesday through Sunday without cost. Beautiful and serene with reflecting pools and arched bridges, the garden is a floral symbol of goodwill between San Jose and its sister city Okayama. Now continue through the park to San Jose Historical Museum, open daily to 4:30 P.M.—admission 25 cents. The museum is San Jose's only exhibition of local history. Awaiting your inspection are wagons, mining tools, early Indian and Spanish objects, farm machinery and a blacksmith shop. You can hear a nickelodeon, see a real flick of the Twenties, and climb on the old wagons.

From the Museum, bike on Phelan Avenue to South Seventh Street. Turn right onto South Seventh to use the bike path down to San Jose State University. At East San Carlos Street, turn right and skirt the campus (no bike riding allowed on campus). Turn right onto South Third Street and bike one-half block to Paseo de San Antonio. Paseo Plaza cuts through the heart of downtown San Jose, three city blocks of urban renewal that is now a parkway with grass, fountains, trees, flowers, and benches. Park your bike and walk up, around, and yes, even through, the two-story high sculptured fountain that is the plaza's focal point. Use the plaza to bike across to Market Street. Turn right to San Jose Civic Art Gallery, 110 S. Market Street. Open Tuesday through Sunday without cost, the art gallery is housed in the historic old Post Office Building and now displays traditional and ethnic art. Docent tours are Tuesday and Friday from 10 A.M. to 2 P.M.

Across the street on the corner of Market and San Fernando Street is St. Joseph's Church. The oldest house of worship in San Jose, it was built in 1877. Admire the elegant old building from the outside, but be sure to park your bike and go inside also. This is a gorgeous Catholic church built in the old cathedral tradition with stained-glass windows, an ornate rotunda, paintings on the walls and ceiling, and beautiful side-altars with flickering vigil lights at the feet of each saint. A booklet of the history of St. Joseph's is for sale in the church office.

Now use Paseo Plaza to ride back to San Jose State, turn left onto Fourth Street and then right onto San Fernando Street. Park somewhere in the area of Fifth and San Fernando and walk into the heart of the campus, using the ivory-covered tower to pinpoint Tower Hall and the fountains which are in the center of the campus. Bike along the north edge of the campus to Tenth Street and turn right onto Tenth past the fraternity and sorority houses which make up Greek Row. Turn left onto William Street for an easy ride to William Street Park at 16th Street. The wooded glen dips down to Coyote Creek, and Olinder Neighborhood Play Center is located here also. Continue on William to 24th Street, turn right onto 24th to pedal back to Keyes and Senter Roads for a total of ten miles. Be sure to leave enough time to take in any attractions at Kelley Park that you missed the first time around.

San Jose Historical Museum
Left: St. Joseph's Catholic Church

Williams Street Park
Lower left: Happy Hollow

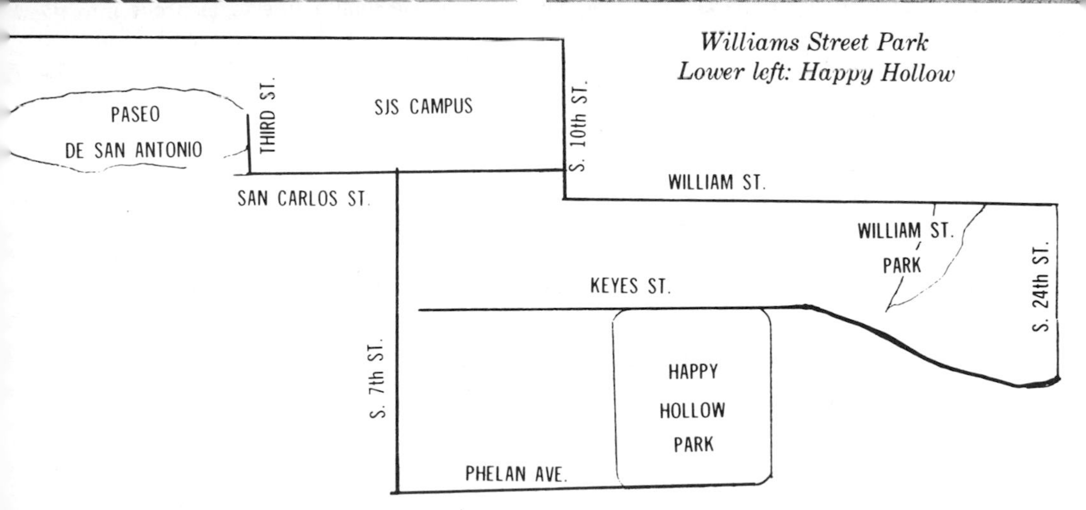

SAN JOSE: Alum Rock Park

Something about Alum Rock Park, deep within the heart of it, is so suggestive of Yosemite that it has earned itself that reputation and description from visitors over the years. Many of them come visiting by bicycle, for bike riders quite naturally take to this softly tree-shrouded park, with deep valleys and steep hiking terrain. From the entrance to the park at the Piedmont and Penitencia Creek Road intersection, the bike trail winds with very little climb to a splendor of towering trees and green cover shrubs. Rustic Lands, the first picnic area on the left, lives up to that name with its isolated setting.

From here the roadway follows the creek, which rushes around rocks and under wooded footbridges. Picturesque and rustic Buckeye Lane, complete with a log cabin, shares the pathway with a stately gazebo.

Young people especially will like to park their bikes to visit the Youth Science Institute Museum, housed at the park. YSI is open Tuesday through Sunday. A colorful thumbnail sketch of park history is given by docents, all volunteers sharing the beauty of this terrain with visitors as they conduct walks through the park. Inside the museum animals are housed, including a white snowy owl and a raccoon which eagerly greets all visitors by reaching out its little paws to shake hands.

County park rangers will happily share the story of Alum Rock Park told in the volcanic action. You can still see a volcanic plug on the hill nearby and other reminders of the violent action that

formed the park. Today green trees arch the quiet stream, animals peek out from the bushes to watch the bike riders pedal by, and road signs at South Rim Trail, Inspiration Point and Quiet Hollow remind the bike riders of another popular way to visit Alum Rock Park—by horseback.

At Alum Rock there are picnic tables, barbecue facilities, and restrooms. There is also play equipment, but youngsters find climbing on rocks, leaping across the creek, and exploring the trails more to their liking.

If you would like to loop out into the Santa Clara Valley flatlands, ride out onto Penitencia Creek Road, following the lazy ribbon of avenue that threads along the creek edge. Turn left onto Capitol Avenue to ride among the strawberry fields and tractors on some of the agricultural land left in San Jose. Now turn left onto Alum Rock Avenue and ride past San Jose Country Club back to the entrance to Alum Rock Park.

Relax and picnic in Alum Rock Park
Left: Alum Rock Creek

Gazebo in Alum Rock Park

PIEDMONT RD.
PENITENCIA RD. ENTRANCE
PENITENCIA RD.
ALUM ROCK PARK ENTRANCE
SAN JOSE COUNTRY CLUB
CAPITOL EXPWY.
ALUM ROCK AVE.

(34) MT. HAMILTON: Huff and Puff and Pedal

One of the most grueling and challenging bike rides in Santa Clara County is the Mt. Hamilton route. This trail is the route of the Pedalera Wheelman's annual Mt. Hamilton Challenge Bicycle Tour. It starts from Lockheed Missiles and Space Co. in Sunnyvale, winds up Mt. Hamilton Road, cuts through San Antonio Valley, and ends in Livermore; total distance is 133 miles. Every year some 600 bike riders turn out, both novices and experienced tour cyclists; it takes about eight hours to finish, and even beginner riders boast that they have passed the "challenge."

You can bike an abbreviated version of this route by going up Mt. Hamilton from the mountain base and then reversing yourself to pedal back down—33 miles each way.

Start at the intersection of Alum Rock Avenue and Mt. Hamilton Road (Highway 130). For those who aren't familiar with the fame of Mt. Hamilton, it is the tallest mountain rimming Santa Clara Valley, the towering peak (elev. 4308) on the south end of the Diablo Range that is often crowned with snow during the coldest days of winter.

The twisting, very steep grade is up, up, up—for 24 miles. The mountain curves and winds and switches back on a twisting track originally designed for a horse-drawn stage. At the summit is Lick Observatory, where powerful telescopes focus on other worlds. Too, there is a village here that is a world within itself, complete with school, a volunteer fire department, a one-man police department, great television reception, and raccoons, deer and an occasional mountain lion as neighbors.

Visitors by automobile, motorcycle or bike are welcome at the Observatory. Astronomers and work crews still man the telescopes, and visitors may view the telescopes and earthquake monitoring equipment, as well as other scientific things in the Observatory, which is part of the University of California system.

Now you have two choices: you can reverse yourself or you can pedal on to Livermore. Only the most experienced riders should consider going on. The route goes through desolate back country that even on a map looks lonely and difficult. The road twists down the far side of the mountain into San Antonio Valley and at Sulphur Creek cuts toward Alameda County, picking up Mines Road. This is an especially pretty section, following Arroyo Macho Creek for miles until the road dead-ends into Tesla Road in Livermore. This entire San Antonio Valley area is referred to as "the back country" and except for an occasional ranch, it is much the same wild country it was when Indians used to pass through the mountains on their way to the sea. From Lockheed to Livermore the distance is 133 miles.

The easiest thing to do from the top of Mt. Hamilton is simply turn around and go back down the same way you came. This route down is a grand downhill sweep into Santa Clara Valley with a marvelous view of the valley and the baylands beyond.

On a clear day, from the top of Mt. Hamilton you can see San Francisco in one direction and Monterey in the other. If it is smoggy or overcast, you can look upwards at the stars instead, through the giant 120-inch telescope which has enriched man's knowledge of the universe.

If you make the pedal with the Pedalera Wheelmen, you get a patch that says "Mt. Hamilton Ascent." If you make it on your own, you merely know that you have done a spectacular ride.

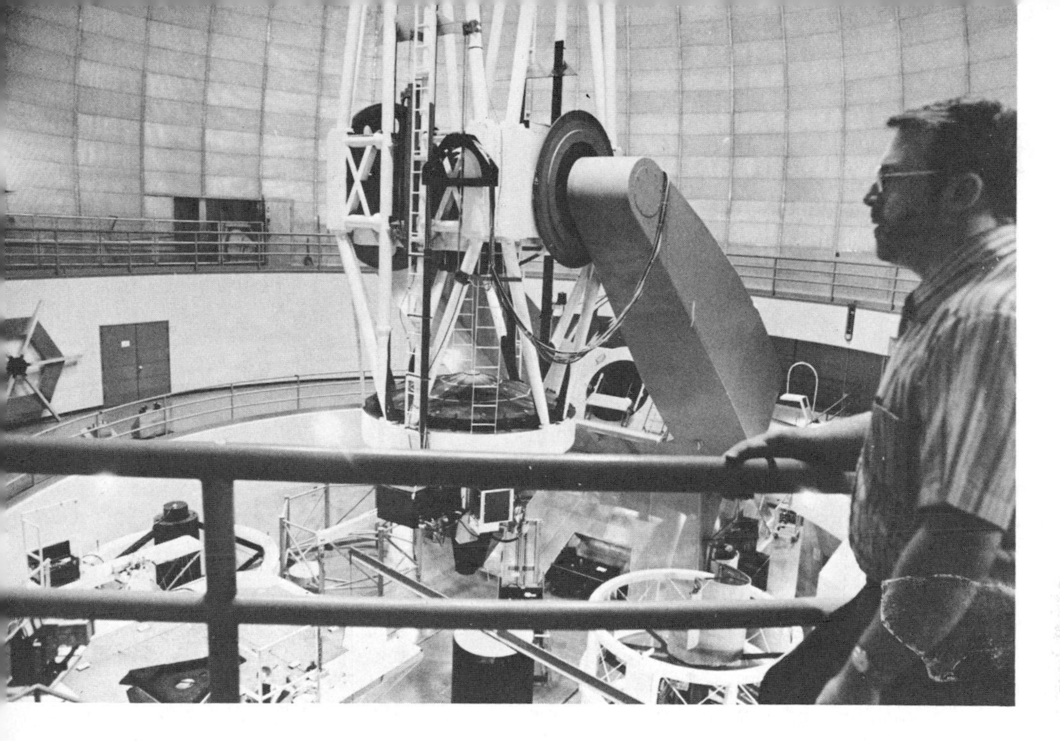

Mt. Hamilton telescope

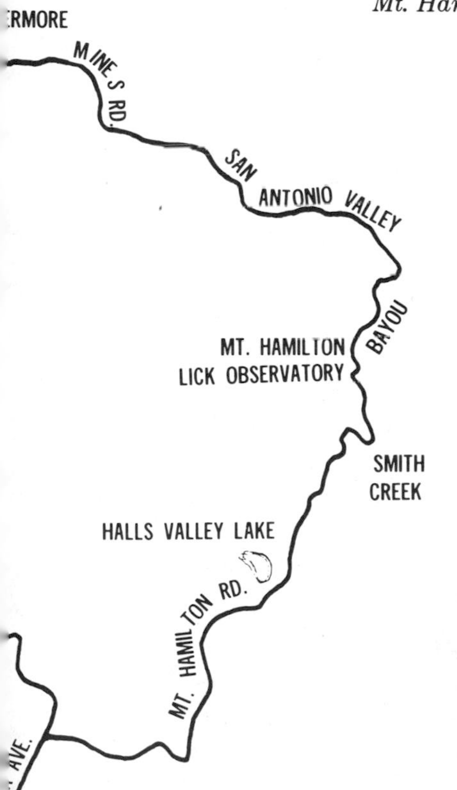

Playground atop Mr. Hamilton

(35) SANDY WOOL LAKE: Uphill and Down

For an uphill battle and a downhill slide, set a date for a bike ride beginning and ending at Ed Levin County Park in Milpitas. The loop covers a mere three-and-a-half miles, but there is a challenge to test your hill-climbing endurance.

Park the car at the park's Sandy Wool Lake. The lake is held in by green mountains on all sides. Even when the valley below is bathing in the summer heat, the park provides a pleasant breeze. Fishermen line the lake; ducks call it home; kite flyers find the breeze just right to tease a kite; kids like to sail model boats on the shimmering surface.

You can explore all around the park by bike; horse and hiking trails crisscross the hillsides and you can bike on any of the paved surfaces. As you bike out of the park, turn right onto Calaveras Blvd. This is the downhill portion and you can use the paved footpath as the bike lane. Turn right onto Evans Road and then right onto Kennedy Drive. There is a fairly steep grade for the first fifth of a mile; after that the incline isn't too difficult. Along here you will see signs of the Milpitas of yesteryear — farms, stables, walnut orchards, and ground squirrels busy at their chores. This is an especially pretty ride in the spring when the orchards wear their colorful blossoms and the wild mustard and acacia add a yellow touch. At the end of Kennedy, turn back up to Downing and the lake.

The park is open from 8 A.M. to sunset. Swimming and wading are prohibited at Sandy Wool, but non-powered boats are permitted on the lake.

The entire park, including the section on the other side of Calaveras Boulevard, covers 700 acres. You can bike over to the other section, using Calaveras, going uphill for a short distance to the stables where horses are for hire. There are picnic sites and another small lake at this end of the park also.

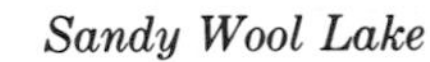

Sandy Wool Lake

Kennedy Drive

SANDY WOOL LAKE
DOWNING RD.
KENNEDY DR.
CALAVARAS BLVD.
EVANS RD.

FREMONT: Along Mission Trail

Discovering Fremont by bicycle is a happy experience. You can use Fremont Central Park as the starting point for an 11-mile loop route through some pleasant biking country with rolling sunburned hills, good biking roadway, some with marked bike lanes, and interesting sights along the way.

Fremont Central Park is located on Paseo Padre Parkway near the Fremont BART Station. At Central Park there is a great playground plus Lake Elizabeth with boats for hire. A swimming pool is at the far end of the park.

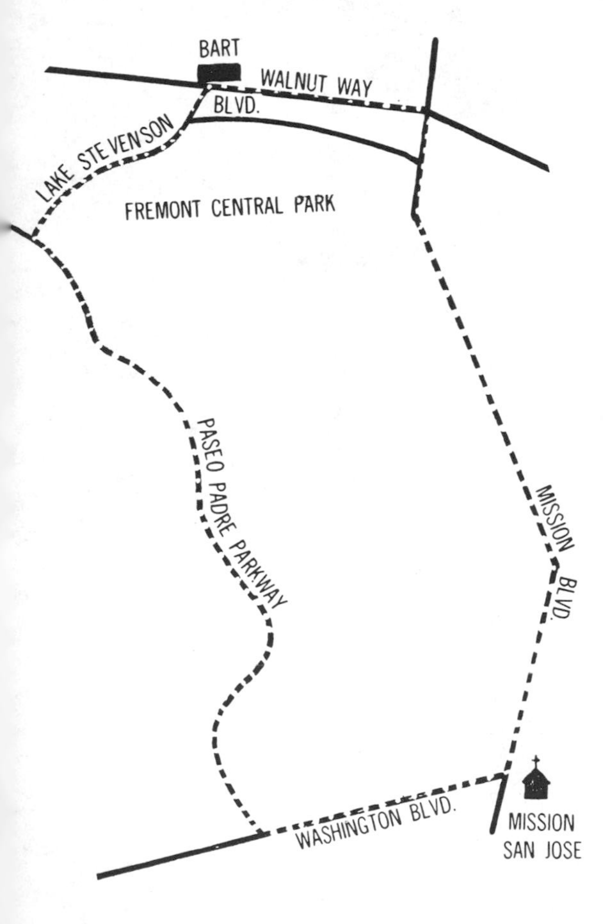

Ride out of the park, turn left onto Paseo Padre and pedal the bike lane that lines the parkway. Turn left onto Washington Boulevard to Mission San Jose, founded in 1797. Despite changes brought by time, the mission bells still ring at Mission San Jose, now part of the city of Fremont. Three of the four original bells that once summoned the Indians to worship hang today in the tower of St. Joseph's Church, the wooden structure built in 1868 to replace the original adobe church destroyed by earthquake.

The adobe buildings you now visit as Mission San Jose are part of the mission monastery. Eight rooms house the numerous artifacts of early California life, and the ninth room is the chapel, with statues carved from wood and salvaged from the old wrecked mission.

The mission is open daily from 10 A.M. to 5 P.M. There is no cost, but visitors may make a small donation to help in the upkeep of the mission.

Along Mission Boulevard across from the mission are some antique shops as well as art shops, gift shops and a cheese-tasting shop for browsing.

Now pedal down Mission Boulevard back toward the foothills. This road is heavily traveled, so use caution. Orchards and rolling grassy hills lend a country flair to this ride. Turn left onto Walnut Avenue and ride down to the BART Fremont Station to watch BART's comings and goings. Youngsters especially would like to lock their bikes here and ride the BART. For the minimum fare, 75 cents, you can ride the BART round trip on the Oakland side of the bay, as long as you don't get off the train.

Now, follow Stevenson Boulevard past Civic Center, turn left onto Paseo Padre and return to Central Park. The park has picnic and barbecue facilities plus restrooms. You can row a boat across the lake, fly a kite on the grassy slopes or take a dip in the park pool.

entral Park Riders, Fremont

Catholic church at Mission San Jose

BART station, Fremont

37

ALVISO: Old but Good

The worn charm of Alviso has become legend. Once a town that rivaled San Francisco as a shipping center for the bay, its canneries, foundries, distilleries and shell works are a part of history.

Today, Alviso is just there. Its streets are pock-marked, its buildings dilapidated. Horses pastured in back yards are ankle-deep in mud. At low tide, boats anchored at the Marina rest on solid ground. "It's a boom town gone bust," say the residents about the now-quiet community off Mountain View-Alviso Road.

But if you look beyond Alviso's disrepaired buildings and rotting boat hulls, you can begin to conjure up imaginings of bygone days. With watchful eyes and an historical map, you can spot the locations that were important in Alviso's heyday and enjoy this unique community bordered by the baylands and slough on two sides and a wild life refuge on a third side. The town is a popular visiting spot for artists, photographers and historians, for many of the old buildings remain untouched. You can ride past the Marina, pedal along the levy that holds back the bay as sailboats glide by, and ride along San Francisco Wild Life Refuge where marsh birds call to each other and only the wind breaks the pattern of the marsh grass.

To enjoy it all by bicycle, take along the accompanying map and spend a day riding through the streets of history. Listed are 21 historic landmarks to see along the way. You may have to feel your way around since some street signs are unrecognizable or missing entirely. Start from the Alviso Marina which is to the right of Point 1.

Where Catherine Street dead-ends into Hope Street, climb the incline to bike along the crest of the floodgate. Sailboats edge along the canal here and this is the route the boats take from South Bay Yacht Club further along the levy. At the corner of El Dorado and Taylor is Vahl's Restaurant, which is reputed to be one of the best dining places around.

If you want to explore beyond central Alviso, pedal out State Street past the church to Spreckels Road. From this point you can look out at the great open space that is the San Francisco Wild Life Refuge (bring your binoculars—the view is terrific). Turn right onto Spreckels and then right onto Los Esteros Street. This takes you through the Alviso residential area back to Taylor Street. Turn right onto Taylor and work your way back to the Marina.

Alviso

Alviso

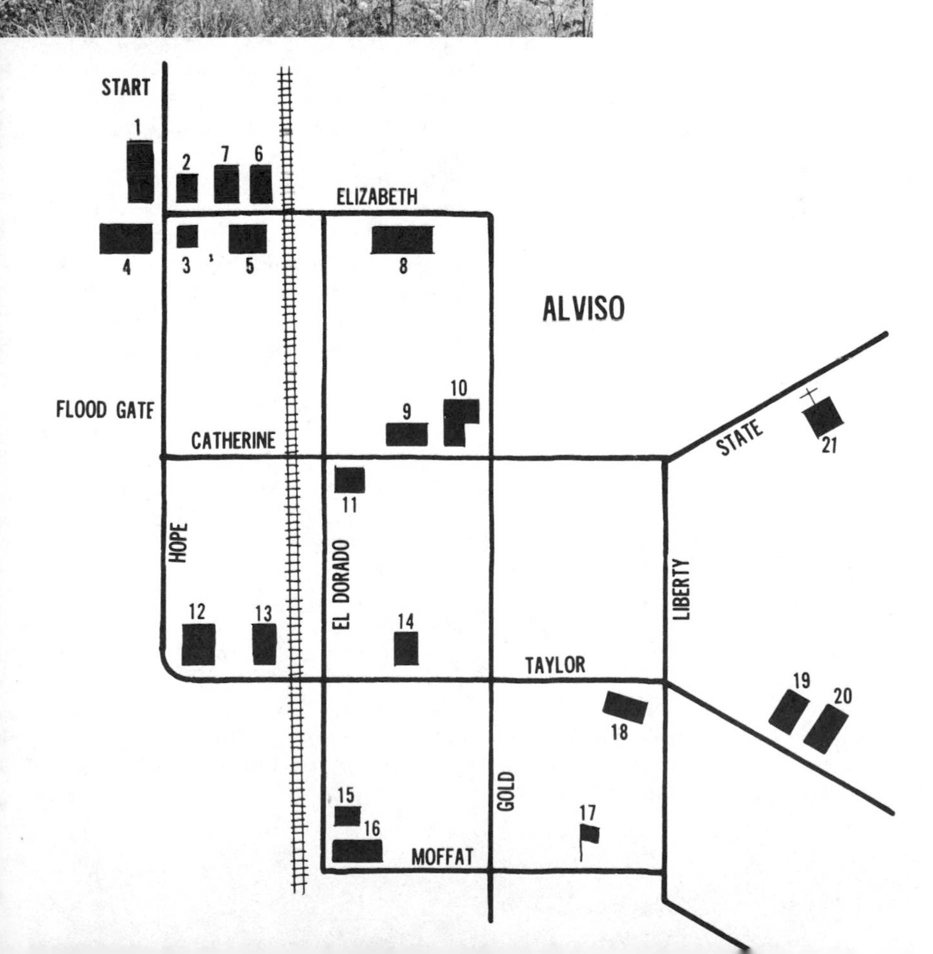
START
1
2
7
6
ELIZABETH
4
3
5
8
ALVISO
FLOOD GATE
CATHERINE
9
10
STATE
21
11
HOPE
EL DORADO
LIBERTY
12
13
14
TAYLOR
18
19
20
GOLD
15
16
17
MOFFAT

(38)

CUPERTINO: De Anza Trek

Cupertino is a ride for all seasons; whatever the time of year, this route is well-suited to a pleasant ride. Start from Memorial Park on Stevens Creek Boulevard at Mary Avenue, across from the north entrance to DeAnza College. Parking is from 8 A.M. to 10 P.M.; there are restrooms, barbecue facilities, a great play area, and sea gulls bathing in the fountain spray of the reflecting pools. Foot bridges span the pools and paths line the waterway. Youngsters will especially like the play area, consisting mostly of well-placed telephone pole-like like pilings for climbing over, crawling through and squirming under.

Bike across Stevens Creek Boulevard to the DeAnza campus entrance. This is one of the most imaginatively-designed campuses in the Bay Area, and it is pure fun to figure a route across the terraced campus. Stop by Minolta Planetarium, the dome-shaped building, which is open Thursday, Friday, Saturday and Sunday for a small admission fee. The solar system seems close enough to touch, with over 100 special effects projectors and the only 27-channel sound system in the United States.

Near the south entrance to the campus is the Cupertino Community Recycling Center, where contributions of glass, metal and aluminum are happily received Friday through Monday from 10 A.M. to 4 P.M.

The south entrance to the campus is on McClellan Road. Turn right onto McClellan and follow the bike path to Stevens Creek. Along here is the heart of Cupertino's history. Juan Bautista De Anza camped beside Stevens Creek in 1776 and his camp is marked by California Registered Historical Landmark No. 800 in the parking lot of Monta Vista High School on McClellan Road. A century after DeAnza, William McClellan led his horses down to water in the creek which spanned his ranch, and the rutted little wagon road he used was incorporated into McClellan Road in 1878.

The site where DeAnza camped beneath the oaks, on the way to establish a presidio in San Francisco, is only a few hundred yards from where the McClellan family settled and from where John T. Doyle established Cupertino Winery 100 years ago. As you pedal along here, the view from McClellan Road has been altered by time and bulldozers, and many of the old landmarks are gone. The thick-trunked sycamores now shade fancy homes and a golf course. McClellan Bridge still spans Stevens Creek, but bulldozers are at work nearby on the old McClellan farm, which will be a new city park. After crossing Stevens Creek, the road winds upward to South Foothill Road.

Turn left onto South Foothill which becomes Stevens Canyon Road. Three possible destinations are before you as you bike up the incline to Stevens Creek County Park.

The first left turn indicates "Buck Norrad Stables" where you can bike down to the horse stables to rent a mount and explore Stevens Creek Park trails by horseback. Horse trails are all over the place and horses definitely have the right of way.

The second left turn off Stevens Canyon Road is at the County Park in the Villa Maria area. The park is open from 10 A.M. to one-half hour after sunset. As you ride down the slope into the park take the left fork, which then climbs up to Villa Maria Picnic Area, where there are restrooms and open spaces for picnicking.

Or you can stay on Stevens Canyon Road to ride up to the third left turn which is Stevens Creek Dam and Reservoir. Walk out on the face of the dam to watch the water dropping over the 120-foot spillway. It is quite a sight. Fishing

con't

Anza College campus

Historic marker in Monte Vista High School

Memorial Park, Cupertino

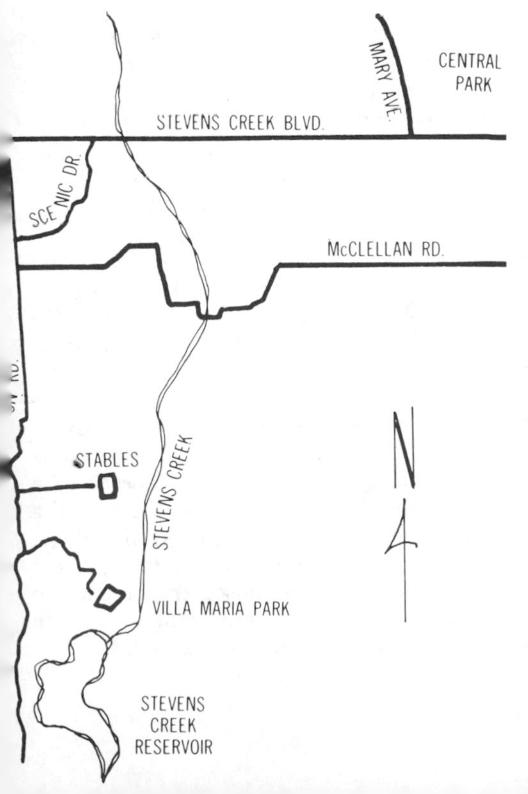

Stevens Creek, Cupertino

FOOTHILL: Hill-Rider's Route

Foothill Community College in Los Altos Hills is appropriately named, for it is on a hill and you have to go by foot. The fact that there are bikes at all on campus only proves how stubborn some people can be. Yet, Foothill campus makes a good starting point for novice hill-climbers. It takes some practice to get used to hill routes, and this one, which winds through Los Altos Hills, is a good one for beginners.

Start by driving all the way around campus to Student Parking Lot T on the highest hill behind the campus. The Space Science Center is located here and you can pedal over to the observatory and Electronics Museum to view the fine exhibits. The Science Carousel has shows on Friday evenings at 8, 9, and 10 P.M. The Electronics Museum is open Monday to Thursday 9 A.M. to 5 P.M., Friday 9 A.M. to 10 P.M., and Saturday, Sunday and holidays from 1 to 5 P.M.

From here ride onto the campus road, turn right and stop at the Planetarium. Shows are given on weekends at different times and the day's schedule is posted on the door. It is downhill all the way off campus to Moody Road. Turn right onto Moody and then right onto Elena Road, which is the first turn you can make off Moody.

Elena Road weaves through pretty residential area with easy hills, from which Los Altos Hills gets its name. There are still some signs of the fruit orchards which once covered these hills. Turn right onto Roblena Avenue and pedal under the Highway 280 underpass. This becomes Burke Avenue as the roadway twists its way past nice country homes cut into the sides of the canyons with oaks and shrubs for shade. There are numerous side roads along here, but stay on Burke and ignore the temptation to explore, since most are dead end roads. Burke comes out in Los Altos at Lincoln Park Plaza along Foothill Expressway.

Bike across Foothill Expressway and take a look at the old Los Altos Railway Station. There is no railroad service to Los Altos today—the old building has been remodeled into a restaurant—but in 1908 both steam and electric lines had hourly service from here and the station was the busiest place in town.

Los Altos' Main Street has numerous crafts and boutique shops, as well as some interesting antique stores, and you can explore the shopping area easily by bike.

Now ride back to Foothill Expressway, cross the Expressway, and turn left to ride south along the route using Lincoln Park Road which parallels the Expressway. There are some pretty stained-glass-window churches along here. Lincoln Avenue follows the Expressway back down to El Monte Avenue. There is an opening through the fence here to bike onto El Monte so that you can use the bike path to ride back to Foothill College. Distance is ten miles; for the last quarter mile, from the campus entrance back to Parking Lot T, you will probably have to push your bike up the steep hill.

Continued from page 78

and boating, but no swimming, are allowed at the dam.

Now bike back down (and it is literally a thrilling downhill race) on Stevens Canyon, turn right onto Palm Drive, named for the towering trees that line this road and sway in the breeze, and left onto Scenic Boulevard. This road follows the creek all the way back to Stevens Creek Boulevard. Turn right onto the Boulevard, pedal through the town of Monta Vista and return to DeAnza College. Total distance is 15 miles.

This is a route suited for all seasons: in the spring riotous colors of wild flowers and new leaves on sycamore and oak color the roadway; in autumn the trees turn brilliant yellow to shimmer in the sun; in summer the canyons are shaded by the oaks; in winter the sun bakes the steep hillsides to warm the canyons and ward off the wind.

Lincoln Park, Los Altos

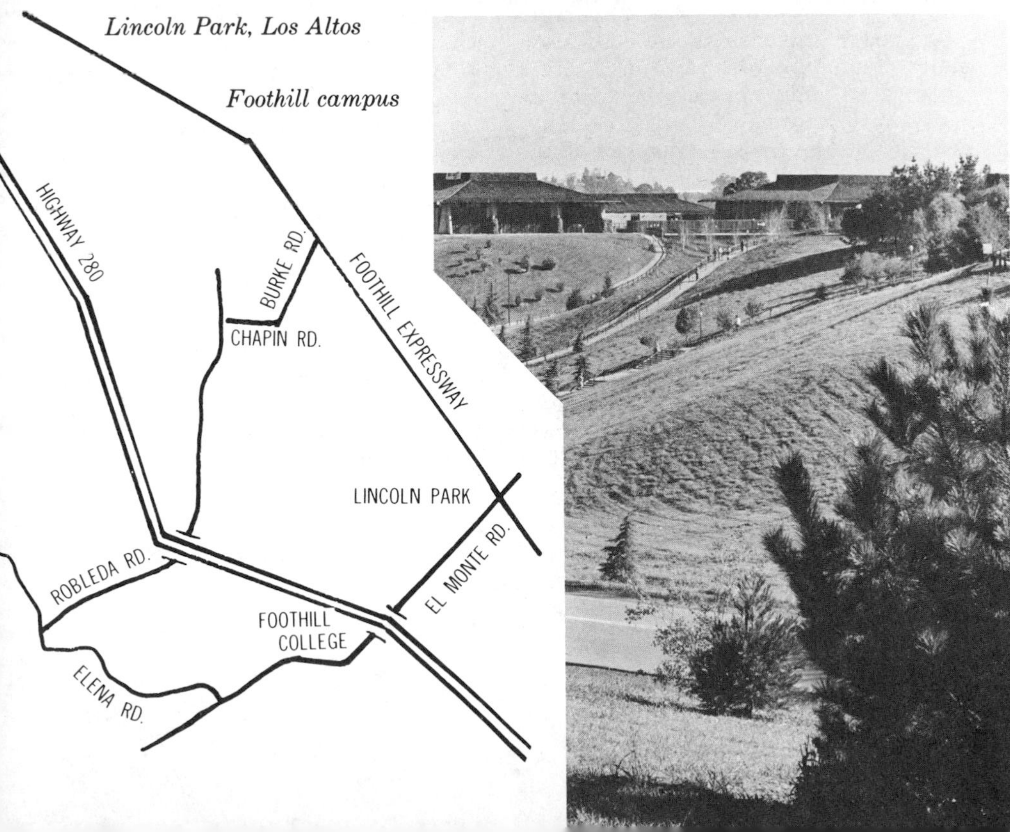

Foothill campus

PAGE MILL ROAD: Around Not Down

Page Mill Road in Palo Alto is a perfect example of a route that is better to go around than down. From the steep hill above Palo Alto, Page Mill Road drops down, down, down for four miles with narrow roadway, blind curves and steep descents that test the bike riding ability of the most skilled riders.

Yet, you can start at the top of Page Mill Road for a round-about ride that weaves through Los Altos Hills and Los Altos and then cuts back to the foot of Old Page Mill Road, a good route that covers 15 miles.

Foothills Park, for residents of the City of Palo Alto only, is located near the summit of Page Mill Road and this is a logical jumping off point for this ride. From the park entrance, take the first right turn onto Altamont Road. This gradually descending roadway runs along a ridge so at times you look right into the oak-dotted canyons of Los Altos Hills, and at times at the stunning view to the left of the San Francisco Bay from Dumbarton Bridge to San Jose. There is one steep decline through a eucalyptus grove before three-mile-long Altamont meets Moody Road.

Turn left onto Moody to pedal past Foothill College. If a bit of hill-climbing seems appealing, loop through Foothill College campus where the Planetarium and Electronic Museum is open Wednesday through Sunday without cost. The world's first radio station, KQW in San Jose, is recreated as it was during its initial broadcast.

Now pedal out the main entrance to the campus, and continue on Moody Road, which becomes El Monte Road as it passes through the Highway 280 underpass. At Foothill Expressway turn left and enter Lincoln Park Mall through the bike opening in the fence at the corner. Pretty grassy slopes, trees and some attractive churches are along here. On Foothill Expressway you can ride much of the way off the main portion of the expressway, on designated bike lanes. Watch the signs for the spot where the bike lane crosses the expressway. In the area of Arastradero Road in Palo Alto, Miranda Avenue parallels the expressway for a safe riding area past the Veterans Hospital.

At Page Mill Road Expressway turn left onto Page Mill Road and watch for the first right turn (about 100 feet) onto Old Page Mill Road. Designated a "recreation route," giant trees form a natural archway along the old road, considered one of the Bay Area's most scenic drives. Along the nearly one-mile scenic route is Frenchman's Tower, a circular brick structure build around 1876 as part of a waterworks.

Bikers, joggers and horses share the traffic over five white bridges which span a creek along this old road. This is a good "pickup spot"; from here, Page Mill Road climbs steadily at a steep incline for four miles back to Foothills Park. Only the hardiest bike riders need try the return climb.

Upper left: Altamont, going up
Above: Old Page Mill Road, Palo Alto
Left: Lincoln Park, Los Altos
Below: Frenchman's Tower, Old Page Mill Road, Palo Alto

STANFORD UNIVERSITY: Campus Tour

Some bike routes have no end—if you are inclined to keep on pedaling—and routes starting from Stanford University in Palo Alto are perfect examples. With Stanford campus as the starting point, you can head in any direction as long and as far as your endurance takes you. You don't even need a map. As long as you keep Hoover Tower in sight you can work your way back to campus.

The map shown here traces a simple six-mile loop from Hoover Tower, around Lagunita Lake, past Stanford Golf Course and Stanford University Hospital, back to Hoover Tower. There are bike lanes all the way, no hills and pretty scenery.

Still, you can improve on this route in a number of ways. As you ride off Stanford campus onto Junipero Serra Boulevard (Foothill Expressway), turn left onto Arastradero Road to ride down to the city of Palo Alto. Use Page Mill Road to work your way back to Hoover Tower.

Or... turn right onto Arastradero Road to pedal into the Los Altos foothills. A right turn onto Deer Creek Road takes you across rolling meadow land to Page Mill Road for a downhill ride back to campus.

Hoover Tower, Stanford campus

Or... as you ride off Stanford campus, turn right onto Junipero Serra Blvd. past Stanford Golf Course to Sand Hill Road. A left turn at this intersection will take you through the hills of Portola Valley to Searsville Lake for swimming, boating and picnicking.

Or... simply stay on the Alameda de las Pulgas from the Sand Hill intersection. The Alameda takes you into Redwood City and as far north as Ralston Avenue in San Mateo, crawling up and down the foothills with pretty views of the bayland on one side and mountains sweeping up to the Skyline on the other. A left turn onto Ralston in San Mateo will head to a hard pedal over the Skyline Route to Half Moon Bay.

Or... if hilly routes are your challenge, turn left onto Woodside Road in Redwood City. Bike through the town of Woodside and see the picturesque wooded area from which the town takes its name. You can loop back to Junipero Serra Blvd. by way of a left turn onto Whiskey Hill Road and then a left turn onto Sand Hill Road near Searsville Lake.

Or... continue on Woodside Road up to Skyline Boulevard—definitely uphill all the way—and turn left onto Skyline. This ride with sweeping views of the Peninsula below follows the mountain crest to Saratoga Gap for a downhill ride to the city of Saratoga.

Or... as you ride off Stanford campus, turn right onto Junipero Serra Boulevard past Stanford Golf Course to Sand Hill Road. A left turn at this intersection will take you on a loop through the hills of Portola Valley. On Alpine Road, use the off-road bike path to pedal downhill back to the golf course and campus.

Stanford Lake

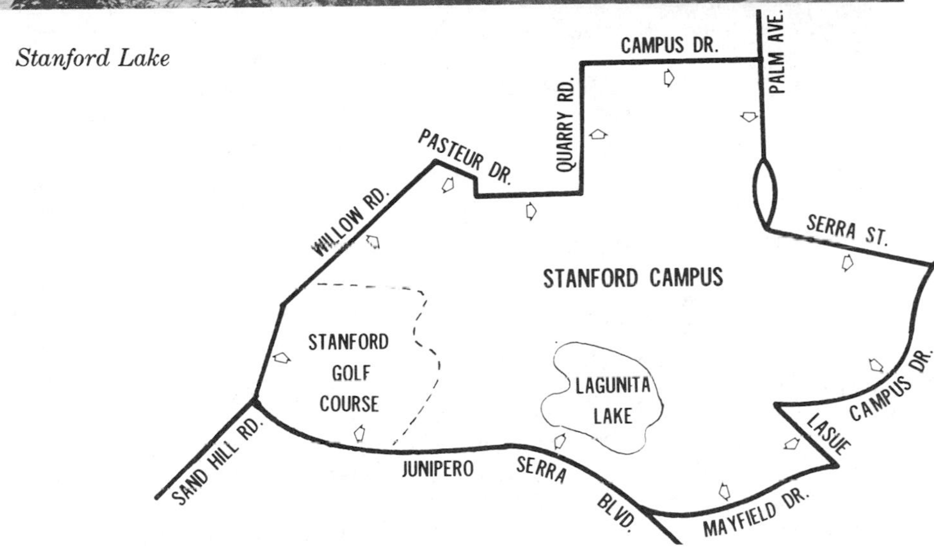

"must-dos" are to view the Stanford Memorial Church, famous for its Biblical murals in mosaic, and a ride to the observation platform of the 285-foot Hoover Tower.

The observation platform of Hoover Tower is open Monday through Saturday from 10 A.M. to noon and 1 to 4 P.M., and on Sunday from 1 to 4 P.M. Stanford Museum of Art is open daily to visitors with docent tours Tuesdays at 2:30 and Sundays at 2 P.M.

The campus is well-suited to biking and pedaling around is the only way the university students manage to cover the huge campus. The tranquil side of the campus is represented by a ride through the Arboretum, a visit to Lake Lagunita, and a picnic lunch in Frost Amphitheater. The best place to meet students, or just people-watch, is around White Plaza. Tresidder Memorial Union contains a large cafeteria, coffee house, bowling alley and a number of different exhibits.

(42)

SAN FRANCISQUITO CREEK: Palo Alto

One of the best routes "designed with bike riders in mind" threads along San Francisquito Creek, the stream that marks the boundary line between the cities of Palo Alto and Menlo Park. Nothing quite compares with biking around Palo Alto because the City Fathers thought about bike riders when they included bike lanes on nearly all its streets, especially the tree-lined ones with their old Victorian houses.

City limits sign

Start at the corner of Alma Street and Palo Alto Avenue near El Camino Real. Palo Alto Avenue begins here to wind its way along the creek through older residential sections with pepper trees, palms and oaks. Along here is a pedestrian-bike bridge that spans the creek into Menlo Park. Pedal across the bridge to come out at the Pacific Telephone Building on Willow Place. Ride through the richly landscaped business park and turn right onto Willow Road.

At the corner is the home of *Sunset Magazine*, marked by the historic El Camino Real Bell in front. Lane Publishing Company delights in welcoming visitors to Sunset, and tour reservations are not necessary unless the group is large. Conducted tours of 50 minutes, through the south building, start at 10:30 and 11:30 A.M. and at 1, 2 and 3 P.M. weekdays. Sunset is closed weekends and holidays.

The buildings are adobe styled in the early mission way with handsome adobe bricks that weigh 30 pounds each. There are stories behind the Navajo rugs, the lamps and benches and even the hand-carved entrance doors which were once the gates of a Mexican hacienda. The test kitchens are part of the visitors' tour.

Sunset's fame, however, rests with its garden. The trees, shrubs and flowers in the permanent garden represent a tour of the Far West from cactus plants and giant yucca plants to rhododendron and azaleas of the Pacific Northwest. Visitors can spend as much time in the garden as they wish without a guide.

Now ride back onto Willow Road and turn right onto Middlefield Road. You must make a quick jog to the left here, crossing Middlefield to pick up Woodlands Avenue, following a road which lines the San Mateo County side of San Francisquito Creek. You can turn back at any one of the streets which cross the creek, or you can continue all the way on a pleasant ride—not a hint of a hill anywhere—that takes you as far as University Avenue at Bayshore Freeway. Now turn back on University Avenue and watch for the first street marking Palo Alto Avenue. This road follows the pretty creek back to downtown Palo Alto.

As you again cross Middlefield Road, watch for Timothy Hopkins Creekside Park. A marker here shows the site where travelers following the mission trail between San Francisco and San Jose used to ford the creek before the first bridge was built in 1852.

Along this section of Palo Alto Avenue back to Alma Street are a number of pretty creekside parks with lawn and trees. The total distance is anywhere from four to 15 miles, depending on the point at which you cross the creek and begin to work your way back.

Bike bridge, San Francisquito Creek

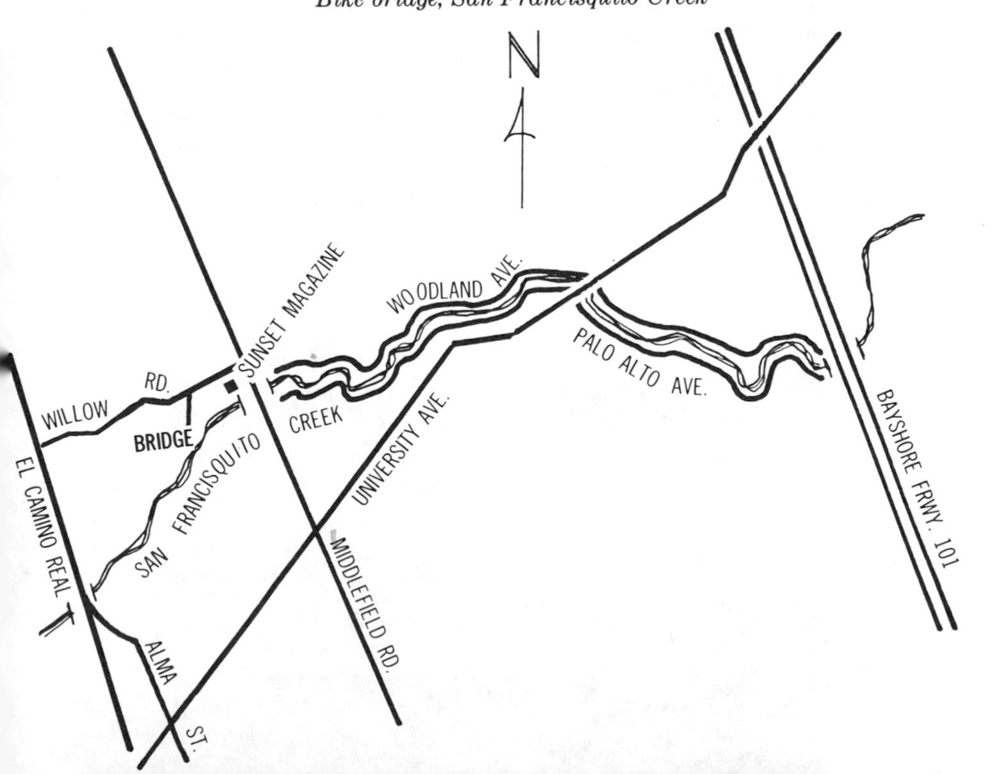

43 PALO ALTO BAYLANDS: Stanford University 88

Access to the baylands is unusual, and access that you can enjoy via bicycle and foot is even rarer. Palo Alto Yacht Harbor and its Baylands Interpretive Center and Nature Walk, open daily to the public, is a delightful starting point for a 14-mile bicycle loop across Palo Alto with Stanford University campus as the halfway point.

Drive to the Yacht Harbor off Bayshore Freeway, taking the Embarcadero Road turnoff. You can bike right up to the front door of the Interpretive Center. Lock your bike and walk the boardwalks across the tanned, golden marshland to enjoy a sweeping view of the San Francisco Bay. Take time to listen; you can see the freeway in the distance, but all you hear are the birds calling to each other and the wind whistling through the marsh growth. A handbook is available at the Nature Center telling about what you can see and hear. Bring along a pair of binoculars. The guided nature walk is at 2 P.M. Saturdays and Sundays.

Now, bike along Embarcadero Road toward Palo Alto. Stop off at Rinconada Park where the entire park complex makes an enjoyable side trip, including the Junior Museum, open daily, and the play area nearby. Especially visit the very pretty Magic Forest here, a stand of giant redwood trees.

Continue on Embarcadero past Town and Country Village. Cross El Camino Real and branch to the right to Palm Drive, the beautiful tree-lined main entry to Stanford University campus. Loop around the Quad to Hoover Tower, the tallest landmark on campus.

Stanford campus itself is a bike rider's dream and you could spend an entire day pedaling around here. Do visit the top of Hoover Tower which is open to the public, see Stanford Memorial Chapel and museum, and view Frost Amphitheater, a spot that will be especially appealing to youngsters.

For the return trip, follow the bike lane along Palm Drive which becomes University Avenue off campus, through downtown Palo Alto. There appears to be more trees than people in Palo Alto and every street is shaded with splendid trees so that the ride along University Avenue is like a trip through meticulously-kept woods.

Cross Bayshore Freeway and turn right onto the frontage road (East Bayshore) to continue back to Embarcadero and then to the Yacht Harbor.

Detour at the Palo Alto Duck Pond near the Yacht Harbor for lunch or a snack, but don't be surprised if the birds come begging. Don't forget to tuck a couple of extra slices of bread in your lunch for the ducks.

Palo Alto Baylands

Busy street (with bikes) in Palo Alto

Stanford campus

YACHT HARBOR

E. BAYSHORE

UNIVERSITY AVE.

EMBARCADERO AVE.

RINCONADA PARK

PALM AVE.

ARBORETIUM

EL CAMINO REAL

HOOVER TOWER

MIDDLEFIELD: Heart of the Mid-Peninsula

Years ago Middlefield Road was just that—a road that ran through hay fields and trees which stretched from Redwood City to Mountain View. Today you can bike Middlefield Road from one end to the other, through the heart of the mid-Peninsula, and still find a few of those fields, along with some other pretty scenes; stately Atherton, tree-lined Palo Alto, industrial Mountain View.

Middlefield Road starts at Veterans Boulevard, off Bayshore Freeway in Redwood City and slices down the peninsula for 20 miles to end at the Central Expressway near Moffett Field.

From the starting point you go through the business section of Redwood City to Atherton and Menlo Park, where beautiful homes and great spreading trees line the road.

Through Palo Alto there are very good bike paths. The City of Palo Alto takes its bike riders very seriously, so this is the best portion of Middlefield Road for bike riders. In Mountain View you can pedal through Mayfield Mall and then pick up Middlefield on the other side.

Old Middlefield ends in the vicinity of Rengstorff Avenue. So turn right onto Rengstorff, go down to the first stop light, and pick up West Middlefield Road. Wide bike lanes border this nice, wide, apartment-lined street with fields in between. West Middlefield goes on and on, crossing Stierlin Road and Moffett Boulevard. Beyond Mountain View-Alviso Road, it cloverleafs into Central Expressway, so it loses its bike-route status.

At any one of the main cross streets in the Palo Alto area, such as San Antonio or Rengstorff Avenues, turn right and pick up Alma Street, which runs parallel to Middlefield. This is the route back as far as the San Mateo County line if you prefer a loop route.

A rider can start and finish at any point along the way, for Middlefield parallels both El Camino Real and Bayshore Freeway, so you can cut into Middlefield by taking any main turnoff from the freeway. One good ten-mile loop ride is from Rinconada Park in Palo Alto to Mayfield Mall in Mountain View and back on Alma Street to Embarcadero Road, on which Rinconada Park is located.

Some interesting sidetrips along Middlefield Road: Flood Park in Atherton; Sunset Magazine and Garden Tour in Menlo Park; Rinconada Park and Junior Museum in Palo Alto; Stanford University in Palo Alto; Mitchell Park Community Center in Palo Alto; Mayfield Mall shopping complex in Mountain View; and San Veron Park in Mountain View.

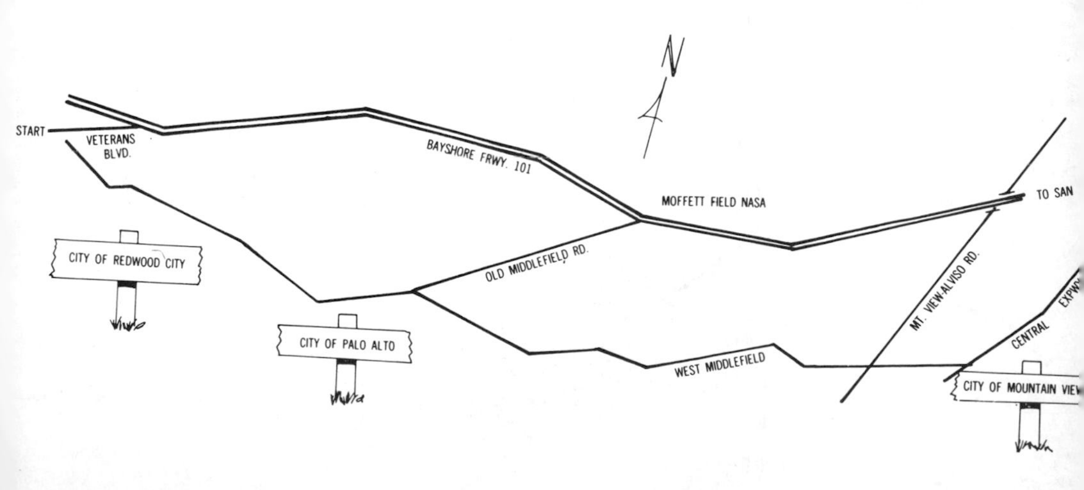

Old Middlefield Way

Middlefield Road

Through Mayfield Mall on Middlefield Road Bike Trail

WOODSIDE: Pedal through the Trees

The logging mills depleted the hills of timber over a century ago so that Woodside became a name, not a fact. But now the redwoods are growing abundantly again. In Woodside and Portola Valley it is an anathema to cut down a tree, and many a roadway or home has stepped aside for nature.

By bicycle you can ride easy roadways that cut through great open spaces of rugged hills, steep canyons shaded by redwoods, and valleys of oak and laurel.

Use the historic old Pioneer Hotel at the corner of Woodside Road (Highway 82) and Whiskey Hill Road as the starting point. This grand old hotel was originally built about 1832 and was restored in the plush Gay Nineties style. Early day loggers found liquid refreshment here on Whiskey Hill Road.

From Pioneer Hotel, ride on Woodside Road toward the Skyline. Great oaks and redwoods shade this path and bikers have to share with an occasional horse or two. Turn right onto Kings Mountain Road where the sign says "Woodside Store." It is one mile along a shaded but narrow road to the store. Woodside Store was built in 1854 among sawmills and redwood groves by Dr. R. O. Tripp who operated the store until his death in 1909. Now Tripp's Store is a public museum, operated by San Mateo County. It is open without cost Wednesday to Sunday (May 1 to Oct. 31) from 10 A.M. to noon and 1:30 to 4:30 P.M. From Nov. 1 to April 30 hours are 1:30 to 4:30. Displays chronicle the logger's life; there are old tools, wood cutting equipment and household items on view.

Now reverse yourself and ride back out to Woodside Road. Turn right onto Woodside to pedal past orchards, corrals and sprawling country homes. For nearly two miles the oaks and eucalyptus trees arch the roadway. The road forks at the point where it begins to climb. Take the left fork onto Portola Valley Road. Along here a marker on the left shows the site of the first sawmill on the banks of Alambique Creek. Brown Sawmill was built in 1847, similar in construction to the famous Sutter's Mill at Coloma. Corraled horses gallop over the site now. Along Portola Valley Road are some great redwood stands and a curious herd of goats in pasture will rush over to watch you pedal by.

At the intersection, turn left onto Mountain Home Road. This is a narrow road; although the inclines are not difficult, caution is advised. At Woodside Road, turn right for a short sprint back to Pioneer Hotel. Total distance is 7½ miles; you can ride this in a couple of hours.

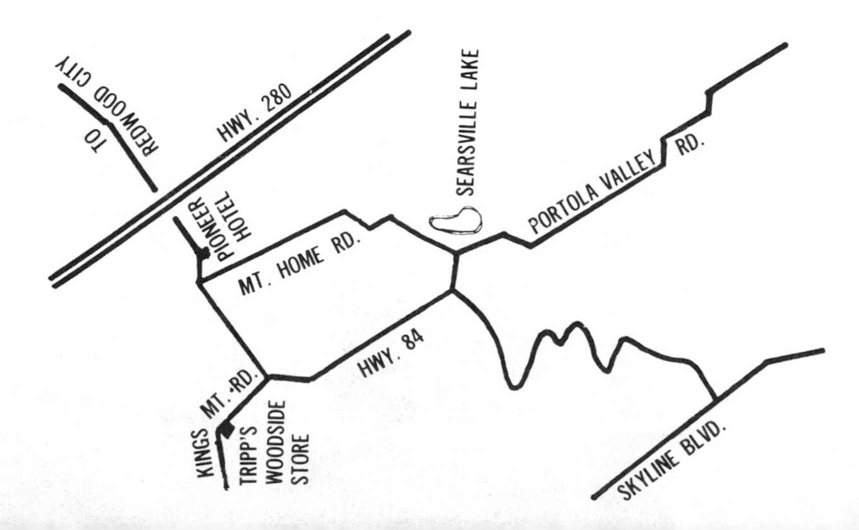

Pioneer Hotel. Built about 1832 and now restored in the plush gay 90s style

Woodside Tripp Country Store, built in 1854

Woodside Store

PORTOLA VALLEY: Lazy Loop

Right-turns-only will take you right around Portola Valley on a 13-mile loop that covers every aspect of the valley's historic past and present prettiness. Start at Searsville Lake where Mountain Home Road meets Sand Hill Road. The town of Searsville was started in 1854 and thrived as a lumbering town until 1891 when the site was covered by water backed up by Searsville Dam. For years, the word Searsville was synonymous with good swimming and sandy beaches; now it is being developed as a biological preserve by Stanford University.

Park your car in the open area near the gate. Turn right onto Sand Hill Road. This is an easy ride through rolling meadowland. Along here you will see a mile-long skinny building which houses the Stanford University atom smasher.

After crossing Highway 280, turn right onto Saga Lane and pedal up the circular drive to Stanford Linear Acceleration Center to the Visitor Center in the Administration Building. Tours are not available on a drop-in basis, but if you call in advance and make reservations, you can be included in one of the scheduled tours. The usual SLAC tour takes about 90 minutes starting with orientation in the SLAC Auditorium and concluding with a guided bus tour of the entire 480-acre facility. To arrange for a SLAC visit, telephone 415-854-3300, Ext. 2204. Shutter-bugs are encouraged to bring their cameras.

Now bike down to Sand Hill Road, turn right and follow the bike path to the busy intersection where Alameda de las Pulgas, Sand Hill Road and Willow Road all converge at Stanford Golf Course. Keep to your right here and you will pedal just a few feet before you turn right onto Alpine Road. Alpine has a terrific off-highway bike-hike-horse trail and you can ride the entire length of Alpine on this nifty pathway, a slight incline climbing to Portola Valley.

Turn right onto Portola Road to bike past Woodside Priory School, numerous stables, horse jumps, a big red Dutch windmill, and a rambling old castle-like stone house with a tower. As you bike downhill into Portola Valley, watch for the historic old Red School House moved to the site when Searsville was flooded in 1891. Along here are signs of Portola Valley's past—its name and the names of many of the roads tell of Spanish origins. There are occasional circles of redwood trees which survived the lumbermill saw. Orchardists and farmers took over the land after the loggers, and their handiwork still stands among the modern day "ranchettes" with corrals and white fences. Altogether it makes a perfectly delightful setting to pedal through; bike lanes and wide roads make this a big lazy loop back to Searsville Lake.

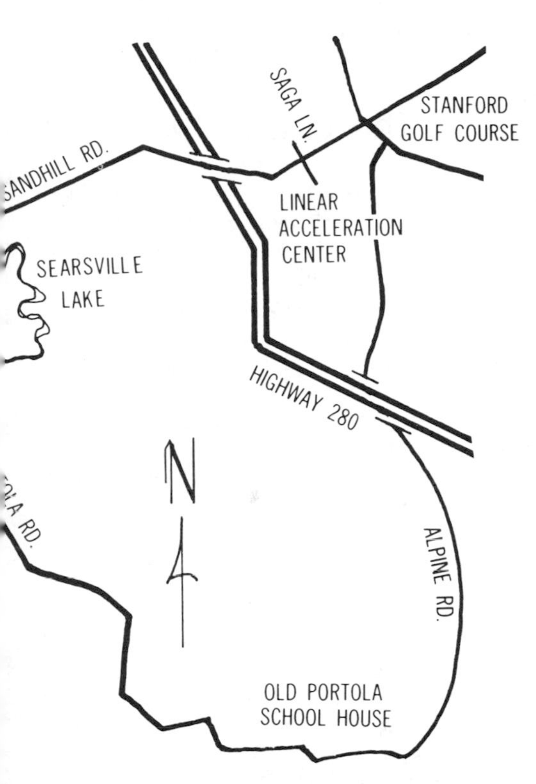

Searsville Lake

Portola Valley Road

OLD STAGE ROAD: Along the Coast

Old Stage Road brings to mind a picture of laboring horses pulling a Wells Fargo wagon up a hill, an accurate picture except that it was the Spanishtown stage, not the Wells Fargo one, that made the rounds of the Old Stage Road between San Gregorio and Pescadero. Today you can bike the same route on a 15-mile loop.

Start at San Gregorio Beach on Highway 1, located ten miles north of Half Moon Bay. The beach is one of the most popular ones along this section, thanks to the nice swimming lagoon at the mouth of San Gregorio Creek, plus a perfect ribbon of sandy beach. From the beach bike up San Gregorio Road and make the first righthand turn onto Old Stage Road. Even on weekends this narrow old road is practically deserted, making it ideal for bike riding. Inclines of this road were carved out with stagecoach horses in mind, and you will find the climb a steady uphill pace not difficult on a 10-speed. There are some fantastic sweeping views of the Pacific surf from the ridges, and in the valleys the green cool farmland is picture pretty.

There are two ridges to bike over. The first one sweeps down to, and then climbs up from, Pomponio Creek. The second ridge extends down to Willowside Farm where you ride under a half-mile arch of twisted eucalyptus trees and through fields where cattle graze. From Willowside Farm, it is a flat ride into the town of Pescadero. This quiet little town looks much the way it did when the stage still used the road. Be sure to stop at the General Store on the main street; it is fun to wander through it and look at the incredible assortment of things offered for sale.

Most people here work the land. The industry is artichokes and strawflowers. If you ride the route in late summer or autumn, you will pedal past fields of yellow, bronze, and orange flowers, stretching from the foothills to the ocean's edge. Stop in at the warehouse of Bianchi Flowers, Inc. on the main street and see how the flowers are packed for shipment to florists for artificial arrangements. As you ride down the road, you will see flats of strawflowers in front yards, laid out in the sun to dry. Women wire the flowers at home and then set them out to dry. Trucks come along later and pick up the dried blossoms.

Turn right onto Pescadero Road and pedal back to Highway 1. At Pescadero Beach, fisherman can be seen casting off the rocks, surf fishing. The catch along here is particularly good. Along here, too, is Pescadero Marsh Natural Preserve. On the right, past Pescadero Creek Bridge, is a hiking trail that circles the marsh. You can easily spot the red-wing blackbird and marsh hawk, as well as sea birds. You can use the foot trail to circle the water and view the marsh without disturbing the wild life.

Traffic along this section of Highway 1 can be particularly heavy on a sunny weekend, but the shoulder of the road serves as a good bike path. You have a short but strenous ride back to San Gregorio Beach, especially if you are pedaling into the wind.

The wind comes from the northwest off the water, so if it is a windy day, reverse your direction on this route. The wind will then be at your back, pushing you along the coast. As you ride the Stage Road, the hills will protect you from the ocean blasts.

Old Stage Route

TO HALF MOON BAY

LA HONDA RD.

SAN GREGORIO

IFIC OCEAN

HIGHWAY 1

OLD STAGE ROAD

PESCADERO

TO SANTA CRUZ

Pescadero Church

(48) PULGAS WATER TEMPLE: Crystal Springs 98

The sign promises "The World's Most Beautiful Freeway"—and while you won't want to bike along that beautiful Junipero Serra Freeway, you can bike a parallel route through Woodside Valley past Crystal Springs Lake and Pulgas Water Temple. Start at the intersection of Edgewood Road and old Canada Road near Canada College in Redwood City. Canada Road is now replaced by Highway 280 so that the road is almost deserted and bikers have an easy pedal over flat terrain with occasional incline. The scenery is unbelievably lovely, for on both sides of Canada is the San Francisco State Fish and Game Refuge.

Turn off Canada Road at Pulgas Water Temple where the classic style temple is surrounded with greenery and a reflecting pool. Be sure to walk over to the water temple and look down at the water rushing through. This water is piped from the Hetch Hetchy Dam in the Sierras to Crystal Springs Lake as the water supply for the City of San Francisco. All along Canada you bike past the Upper Crystal Springs Reservoir surrounded by grassy fields and stands of eucalyptus. An interesting story is that the San Andreas Fault runs along the floor of the lake and you can actually trace the fault line by noting the lowest point of the valley beyond the reservoir.

As you come to the freeway interchange, watch on the right for the sign indicating a paved bike path to Ralston Avenue. This takes you under the freeway to Ralston, over a small incline and down into the town of Belmont. Turn right onto Alameda de las Pulgas to wind along the lower foothills past San Carlos High School into Redwood City. When you reach Edgewood Road, turn right and climb over the last hilly portion for the downhill sweep to Canada Road, for a seven-mile loop route.

If you would like to add on five more miles, stay on Alameda de las Pulgas through residential Redwood City. Turn right onto Woodside Road. You begin an incline at Menlo Country Club that goes uphill all the way to the town of Woodside. At the Pioneer Hotel, turn onto Canada Road and pedal past the ranches and country homes back to Edgewood Road.

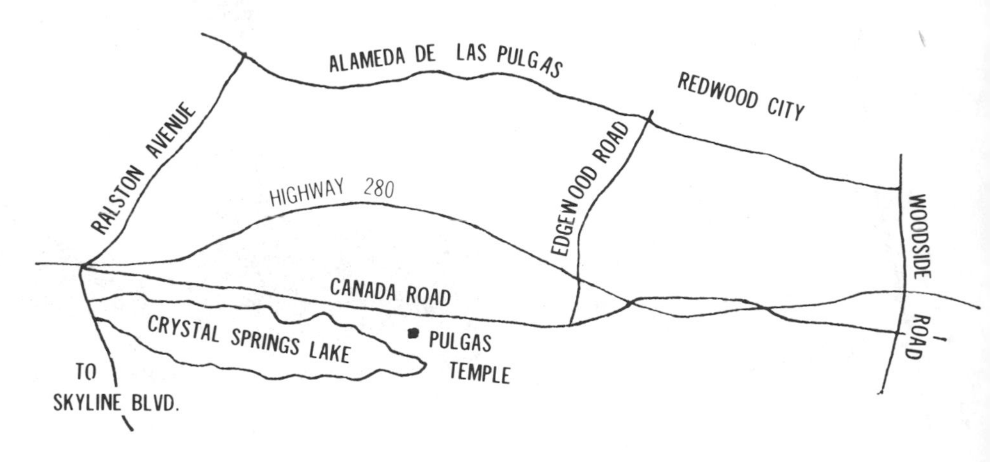

Upper: Alameda del las Pulgas through Eucalyptus grove, San Carlos

Lower: Pulgas Water Temple

Top: Crystal Springs Lake
Middle: Pulgas Water Temple
Bottom: Crystal Springs Point

49

SAN FRANCISCO: Bike the Bay

San Francisco by bicycle might sound like a hill-climber's nightmare; still, it is one of the best bike tours around. This very fine ride crosses the Golden Gate Bridge and returns to San Francisco via the Sausalito Ferry.

Beginning bike riders find this route vigorous, but not impossible. There is some hill climbing; it only means getting off and walking uphill a distance. A fog-free day is nice, but not a necessity to enjoy this ride.

Start at the Golden Gate Bridge toll plaza where you can park free for six hours, allowing ample time for the loop route of 18 miles by bike and eight miles by ferry. There is no charge to ride across the bridge.

The easy pedal to the Marin side permits a chance to watch the bridge workers. Autos whip across the span, outgoing ships glide beneath the bridge, the fog horns moan overhead, and the San Francisco skyline and Alcatraz sweep before you.

Bike route signs direct the rider under the bridge to the long downhill grade to the shore of Fort Baker. Usually it is surprisingly sunny along the sheltered shore, for even on foggy days the sun manages to break through in Sausalito. Marvelous little shops and cliff-hanging homes line the way along the Sausalito waterfront on Bridgeway Drive. There are a number of good restaurants here; better yet, try one of the carry-out sandwich shops (they will build any Dagwood combination for you) and sit on the sea wall to watch the sailboats on the bay.

The Golden Gate Ferry docks near the park area and the trip by boat is fun. Cost is 75 cents for adults and there is no extra charge for wheeling your bike aboard. In fact, the ferry does a regular business with "bike commuters." On weekends it can be crowded, so you might have to wait for the next boat.

The ferry docks at the Ferry Building on the San Francisco side. Pedal northward on the Embarcadero along the waterfront, past freighters loading cargo for ports. The Embarcadero takes you to Fisherman's Wharf, then past Ghiradelli

con't

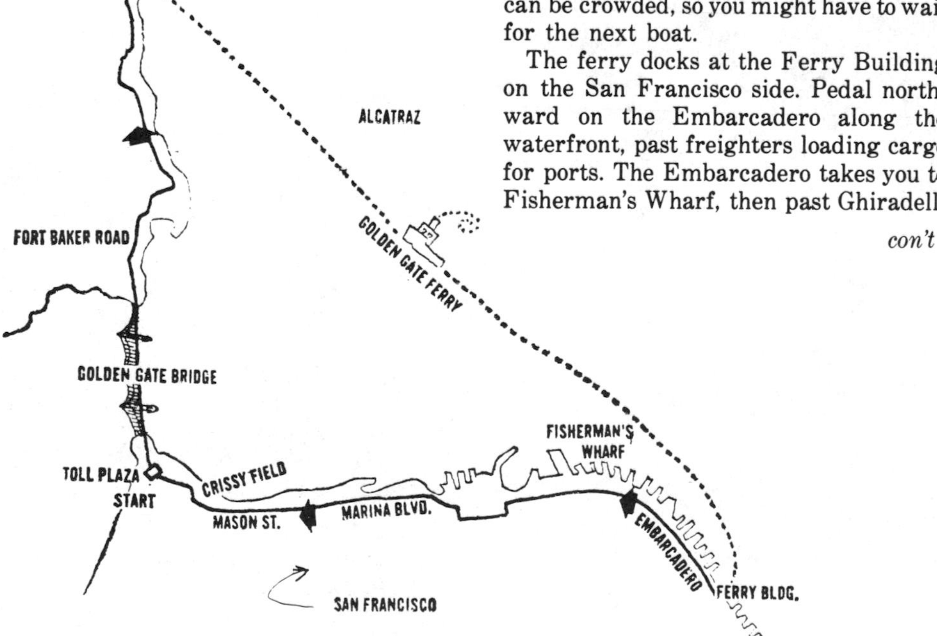

Bridge, San Francisco to Sausalito

Upper left: Sausalito ferry to San Francisco

Left: Sausalito bike route

Below: Sausalito

Square and wherever your handlebars direct you. The Golden Gate Promenade for example, takes you through Fort Mason to the Marina Green where sailboats fight the afternoon wind. Turn up Mason Street to the Presidio.

If you aren't familiar with San Francisco streets, simply follow the bike route signs from the San Francisco Maritime Museum. This takes you up two hills and then over a relatively flat route that gradually works uphill past the Palace of Fine Arts to the Presidio.

Stay on Lincoln Boulevard, the main road through the Presidio Army Base. Crissy Field Avenue dips under the freeway to come up on the bay side. From this point it is strictly uphill and you must push your bike back to the bridge toll plaza.

SAN FRANCISCO: Golden Gate Park

The most satisfactory way to really see Golden Gate Park is by bicycle. It is not an accident that bikes are so popular in the park, for you can bike from one end to the other on 15¾ miles of roadway and see every one of the sights; nowhere, except on footpaths, are bikes prohibited.

Ten-speeds abound. So do the popular bicycles-built-for-two which can be rented at bike shops located near the east and west entrances. The real fun of biking Golden Gate Park is that you are able to discover quiet little spots that no one else appears to know about. There are all kinds of delightful nooks and crannies—secret gardens, tiny bridges and bright flower patches that only you and the gardener and the tree squirrels have found. If you can resist the temptation to see the Japanese Tea Gardens and the aquarium this time around, you will find more time to bike to the lesser-known spots.

You can bike the whole park from the ocean beach on one side to Stanyun Street on the other; or you can park anywhere within the park, unload your bike and pedal off to see whatever appeals to you.

For the entire park ride, start at the Beach parking area at the Great Highway and pedal onto South Drive to enter the park. Right off you are in the pine and cypress shade of the park. Whatever the season, flowers add bright splashes of color, little lakes give cool accents, and the horticultural miracles that make up the park are seen everywhere.

Across 19th Avenue is the best known part of the park—and the most traveled, for tourists and autos are everywhere. In quick order you come to Strybing Arboretum and Botanical Gardens, the Japanese Tea Gardens, deYoung Museum, and the Academy of Science. A bike is most welcome here because you can maneuver around those autos and tourists, park your bike at each attraction, view to your heart's content and then get on your bike

con't

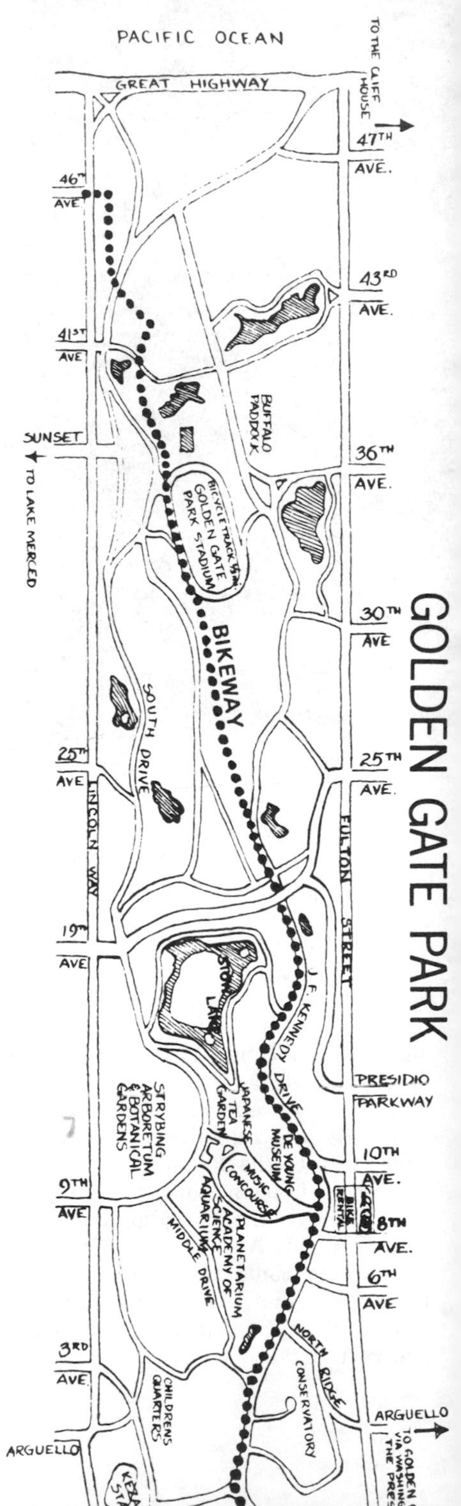

In Golden Gate Park:
At top: Stow Lake; above left: Japanese Tea Garden; above right: bikers; left: joggers.

Conservatory, Golden Gate Park

and ride to the next one. Most places are open from 8 A.M. to 4:30 P.M. daily. Only the Academy of Science charges a small admission fee of 50 cents; all others are without cost.

Stay on South Drive to loop around Strybing Arboretum onto 9th Avenue. Veer to the left off the main drive (keep your eye on the 49-Mile Drive signs; they are good guides) to the Bowling Green and Playground. Don't pass up the fascination of watching the lawn bowlers in action. This road runs into John F. Kennedy Drive at the Conservatory of Flowers. The great dome-shaped glass building is as curious inside as outside. Built in the same style as the Conservatory in Kew Gardens in England, the one here is open daily with guided tours of the tropical gardens and flowers.

Head back toward the beach on JFK Drive. Along here there are no crowds and by bicycle you can see some of the lesser-known garden spots. You may be the only person exploring the almost-hidden Fuchsia Gardens and Camellia Gardens (use North Ridge Road, which loops behind the Conservatory), or the lone admirer of the John McLaren Rhododendron Dell where great pines shade the gorgeous blossoms (beyond the Conservatory at 6th Avenue).

On the left off JFK Drive is Stow Lake, the park's best-known lake, where there is a snack bar, and boat rental is available. You can bike around Stow Lake on the roadway, but the footpath is for walkers and joggers only. Your return trip to the beach takes you past some smaller ponds, open meadow, the buffalo paddocks and the golf course. Total mileage is about 15 miles, depending on how much you explore; the ride is easy-paced and even beginning bikers can go the whole route.

In addition to the bike route following the two main roads, there is a bike ride that cuts right through the heart of the park for three miles. Part of the Master San Francisco Bike Route, it follows the bridle path from 46th and Lincoln Way across the park to pick up JFK Drive at 19th Avenue. It continues to Stanyun at Fell Street. For a copy of the map, "Golden Gate by Bike," or the Golden Gate Park brochure, write to San Francisco Parks and Recreation, McLaren Lodge, Golden Gate Park, San Francisco, CA 94117, requesting them by name.

Bikers have the best time on Sundays. On that day, JFK Drive from 19th Avenue to Stanyun is closed to motor vehicles. Bikers and joggers have the right-of-way. If you ride the park any other day, be sure to start early to avoid the late-afternoon bike jam in the park.